The Fear of Singing
Breakthrough Program™
Learn to Sing Even if You Think
You Can't Carry a Tune!

Nancy Salwen

Music All Around
Keene, New Hampshire

Published by Music All Around
Keene, New Hampshire
www.musicallaround.net
www.fearofsinging.com

The Fear of Singing™ Breakthrough Program:
Learn to Sing Even if you Think You Can't Carry a Tune!

First Edition
Printed in the United States of America

The exercises in this book are given as suggestions and are to be done at your own discretion. The author assumes no risk.

Some of the names and details of singing students have been changed to protect their privacy.

Editing support team:
Marcia Passos Duffy, April Leighton, Dorian Zimmerman, and Kim MacQueen.

Recording Engineer: Ben Rogers, Loud Sun Studios. www.loudsun.com.

Cover design and book layout: Salwen Graphic Design.

Illustrations copyright: Nancy Salwen and Kristina Wentzell.

About The Fear of Singing Breakthrough Program

The Fear of Singing Breakthrough Program is an accessible, user friendly, and inspiring book for those afraid to sing as well as experienced and professional singers. It is a remarkable guide through the process of rediscovering the profound genius of the authentic singing voice that exists within each of us.

For those just beginning to step bravely into the world of singing, this book provides a clear, comprehensive, and supportive guide toward getting over internal doubt and fear and making the journey into the transformative possibilities of the human voice. For experienced and professional singers, this book is a brilliant reminder as to the sheer joy of authentically reconnecting with singing for the sake of celebrating life in sound!

Nancy has given us a great gift by creating a book that will most certainly not only inspire you but will provide you with all of the support needed to discover or rediscover the extraordinary and unique singer within each of us!

— *Mary Knysh*
  Founder of Rhythmic Connections
  Teacher/Trainer for Music for People

From personal experience I can happily say that Nancy is a one-of-a-kind teacher. Her skill, personality, thoughtfulness, and warmth are unmatched as she guides and supports her students through the process of reclaiming his or her voice. She can help even the most timid non-singer feel safe to experiment.

With kindness, playfulness, and heart, Nancy will help you explore your voice and reclaim the joy and courage we all had singing as children. I'm so happy to now add her book to my library. Thank you, Nancy!

— *Shendl Diamond*
  LikeMinds Press

Nancy Salwen's unique and inviting approach to getting us past our fears about singing will, if we allow her to guide us in her wise and warm manner, lead us out the other side of fear, and into joy!

Nancy takes the mystery out of music theory by gracefully dismantling it into understandable units that we can readily grasp and use to find our voices.

At last, those of us who thought our voices might never emerge can develop our vocal instruments and be heard well beyond the confines of our shower walls!

— *Ed Tomey*
  Leadership Consultant & Executive Coach
  Keene, NH

This book is dedicated to my mother, Milly Basser Salwen,
who lived a courageous and adventurous life despite
her fears, and gave so much to so many people.
Thank you Mom, for bringing me to folk festivals and
peace marches, for keeping an eclectic collection of
instruments from all over the world on top of our piano,
and for always being an improvisor in all ways
as well as a lover of community music-making.
And thanks for never objecting to my constant singing —
that in itself was an amazing gift!

And for Eula, Eva and Ann
with so much love.

Foreword

I vividly remember the first voice lesson I ever taught. It was a warm August day in 1993. My student, a middle-aged medical diagnostics lab technician, was eager and ready to learn. With my limited knowledge and intuition, I began the journey with him. Two years later, this same student released a CD, and raised a considerable amount of money for a local hospital.

Since then I have continued to teach singing to people of all ages and levels in a wide variety of settings. I have witnessed, and continue to be touched by the many ways in which recreational singing enriches people's lives. Some people just sing their favorite songs at home while others join community choirs and amateur musical theatre companies.

Although we value vocal beauty, virtuosity, and artistry, being a high level professional is not what singing is all about. If we consider the large role that singing has played in every single culture for thousands of years, we immediately regain the bigger picture. Research has proven that daily practice of singing offers physical, emotional, cognitive, and social benefits.

I met Nancy Salwen, creator of *The Fear of Singing Breakthrough Program*, several years ago at a Music For People "Art of Improvisation" workshop. I was new to Music for People, and had just started their four-year Musicianship and Leadership Program. My first encounter with Nancy was purely musical. Before we even had a chance to say hello, we were singing together as part of an ensemble. I still remember how her sincere smile and naturally expressive voice put me at ease. During the course of that weekend, I learned that she was two years ahead of me in the program. I got to know Nancy as a colleague, musician, and person. Nancy is an inspiring, musical, creative, warm, down-to-earth being who lives to share her deep connection with music and love of singing with others. Her book is a must-read for anyone who wishes, longs, or lives to sing (including pro singers and voice teachers). While the book provides support to those who believe they cannot sing, it will also touch every singer, regardless of level of experience.

Realistic and genuine, Nancy, who comes from a folk music background, addresses fear of singing in a straightforward manner that speaks to everyone. Her writing is from the heart, and her knowledge is experiential; her range of teaching and singing experience shines through in this approachable and interactive book. Her ideas are easy to follow, and her sensitivity to varied learning styles is evident in the layout of the book. Those who love to read a book from cover to cover will find lots of useful information, and those who prefer to jump right in and try things will find handy lists, exercises, and tips. She breaks down the skills of singing and helps readers recognize the skills they already have.

Thank you Nancy for creating an innovative book that I am sure will inspire many.

Dr. Irene M. Feher, D.Mus.
Professor of Classical/Contemporary Voice at Concordia University in Montreal
Voice teacher, performer, improvisation facilitator, and speaker.
livingyourmusic.com

The Fear of Singing Breakthrough Program
Table of Contents

Every particular in nature, a leaf, a drop, a crystal, a moment of time is related to the whole, and partakes of the perfection of the whole.
- Ralph Waldo Emerson

So it is with every human voice.

Meet Your Guide

I have always loved to sing. I am not, however, a musical prodigy, or oozing with talent. I'm guessing you aren't either. I used to be afraid to sing in front of other people. I suffered (and still do, to some degree) from extreme stage fright.

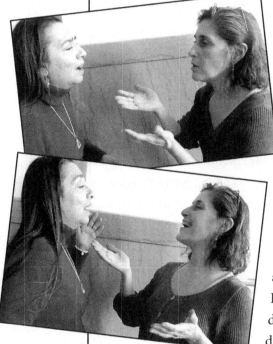

What made this so sad was that although nothing moved me the way singing did, I let my fear stop me from pursuing it. Many people, even "non-singers," have a passion to sing. And many people feel stuck or hopeless about their fear of singing. Does this sound familiar? Maybe we have something in common!

The great news is that I have found ways to move past my fear and now experience great joy from singing in my life, and I know that you can, too.

In addition, because singing is an activity that touches us so deeply, dealing with our fear of singing provides an opportunity to change how we relate to all our fears. Becoming comfortable with your singing voice has a delightful way of flowing into other areas of your life. It did for me; it can for you. More great news!

Singing in some contexts came naturally to me. I sang my bunkmates to sleep at night with lullabies at summer camp. I sang as I walked down the street or waited for the subway as a kid growing up in New York City. As a teenager I took classes in Balkan singing and discovered the joy of singing in harmony and the richness of singing the songs of another culture. As a preschool teacher I led songs for classrooms full of children, no problem. But, as soon as I stepped onto a stage, saw the microphone, and looked out at the audience, I could barely get a note out. My voice shook uncontrollably; I couldn't wait to get off the stage.

While I had fantasized all my life about a career in music, this fear of singing in public stopped me in my tracks. Instead, I turned my attention toward visual art, became an art major in college, and chose a career as a graphic designer. In a sense I'd given up, yet I didn't let singing go entirely.

Although I didn't like performing, I didn't stop singing altogether, or relegate myself to singing alone in the shower or the car. I loved singing with other people casually, jamming at parties or whenever opportunities arose. I went to singing workshops and multicultural singing camps. Finally, in my 30s I joined a chorus and found that performing, as long as I was part of a group, wasn't so scary for me.

Through the years, other singing opportunities came my way, and saying "yes" (even though I was scared to death) helped me come upon the discovery that changed my life: I absolutely love to teach other people how to sing.

After a particularly moving experience at a week-long multicultural singing camp (with an organization called *Village Harmony*), I decided it was time to finally take action towards becoming a song leader. I took harmony-singing lessons, developed song leading skills, and became certified by an organization called Music Together as an early childhood music educator. I began teaching music classes for kids and their families. I started teaching music classes in preschools. Soon after, I started giving private lessons to adults. In this context I wasn't afraid (I was jazzed) and music was becoming my life.

Many people want to sing but close the door on that wish because they are afraid and discouraged (much the same way I shut the door on singing as a career for many years because of my stage fright). I realized that if I could overcome my fear of singing, I could teach other people to do the same. I could see clearly the ways that my students' fear was impeding their ability to learn even the basics of singing; fear got in their way of focusing, from being able to listen very well, and from using their voices freely and comfortably.

I designed and ran my first Fear of Singing workshop in 2010 with this in mind. I used techniques in the workshops that I had developed along the way to overcome my own fear … tuning into body awareness, listening in new ways, connecting to the meaning of the song I was singing, and connecting my voice to my emotions.

The workshops were a blast, and also deeply moving. Being in a room full of people willing to take a chance, step beyond their fears, and share their voices with each other is a profound honor. The participants feel it too and support each other in beautiful ways. The practice of accepting others in their imperfection helps each person accept their own imperfections. It's hugely liberating to realize that it's okay to sing with other people even if you're not perfect! Once they got past the fear, they could dig into learning and practicing the skills of singing, and start to understand how songs work. While the workshop participants began to discover their inner singer, shared their voices with each other, and learned important singing skills, I became clear that this was the direction I wanted to go with my life and career.

When a student says they finally feel comfortable enough to sing lullabies to their children, or says, "I sang the 'Happy Birthday' song for the first time!" my heart sings. When someone tells me that after a lifetime of considering themselves a non-singer they have joined a community chorus, I know I'm doing the work I'm meant for. This is my love and joy.

Since not everyone can attend my workshops, I wrote this book to bring the joy of singing to more people. By using the techniques outlined in this book along with the tracks and videos on the accompanying website, you too can move past your fear and begin to enjoy your singing voice in new ways.

When non-singers learn to sing, they often change their relationship to singing — and other aspects of life as well — from one of fear, apprehension and avoidance to one of strength, courage and love. This is what I wish for you.

How to Use This Book

This book is your guide to a program designed to help you learn to sing and to feel more confident about singing. It's fully customizable to fit your needs, your learning style and the realities of your daily life.

Photo, Herman Chanania, 1987. Mazi Cohen singing at the Jewish Arab Rally for Peace and Coexistence at Neve Shalom.

Do it Your Way!
• You can read the book front to back doing all the exercises as you go along, or,
• You can start with the Table of Contents, skim the whole book, and then just use the parts that are most relevant to you, or,
• You can jump right to the exercises at any time.

The Exercises
There are exercises in many of the chapters to help you gain and practice the skills you need to sing, and to help you work through your fears about singing. Many of them incorporate writing, listening to audio tracks and watching short videos. Do the exercises with a sense of exploration — they're designed to be fun!

The Audio and Video Tracks
For the exercises that have audio and/or video tracks associated with them, go to www.fearofsinging.com/book1. Because you've purchased this book you will have access to the content there for free. It's a great idea to have the audio tracks available when you're in the car, on the subway or bus, taking a walk or washing the dishes — so consider burning a CD from the tracks on the website or downloading them so that they're available to you on a portable device.

Throughout the book the following symbols will alert you to audio tracks and videos:

audio   video

Handy Dandy Warm-Up Sheet and List of Practice Ideas
You may find it useful to have an at-a-glance reminder of techniques and exercises to help with learning and practicing. On Pages 227 and 229 you will find lists that you can copy and put into a handy place for reference. You can also download them from the website. These will help you with your ongoing practice.

Tip

Hey Look! The Website address is at the bottom of almost every page of the book!

Finding Time and Space for Your Practice

It is important that you find a way to make this program work for you and your life-style. At first you may need to devote chunks of 10-20 minutes or more to each exercise. Give yourself enough time to settle in and become familiar with the exercises. However, as you progress you can decide how much time you want to spend with any given exercise. Ideally you'll give yourself enough time to "get into the zone." Some of the exercises might bring up emotions, and you'll want the space and time to process them. Or, you may find that you're able to get value out of spending even just a couple of minutes on an exercise you're already familiar with.

Conversely, there may be exercises that deeply resonate with you, and you may want to take more time with these. Be sure to create opportunities for yourself to delve and explore!

You may want to do your exercises in private. You will be exploring your voice, and knowing that others can hear you may be inhibiting. Be sure to find situations for practicing that feel comfortable and emotionally safe.

Journal Pages

To get the most from this program, you will be writing, either in the pages of this book or in a separate journal. Some of the exercises explicitly include writing as a way to process your thoughts and feelings. Think of your journal or pages as a travel companion on your singing journey, a place where you can explore strong feelings, an interesting insight, or a question. Keep a pen or pencil handy during your exercise sessions!

Beyond the Book

For some of you this book will provide everything you need to discover your inner singer, but for others this may be just the beginning. If you want more and different kinds of support, please visit www.fearofsinging.com for online programs, in-person and Skype singing lessons, and workshops. In addition, Chapters 22 and 23 are full of great ideas on how to keep yourself growing as a singer once you've completed this program, including ways to connect with other people to sing with in your community.

Why Don't the "How-To-Sing" Chapters Come Earlier?

This is not just a how-to book. If the title of this book was "Learn How to Sing," and it was not specifically geared towards inexperienced or fearful singers, I might have started you out with the Matching Pitch exercises in Chapter 14. But because singing is so emotionally challenging for many people, we need to focus on other things first.

I want you to think about why you're scared to sing, and begin to dismantle that fear; I want you to work with your body and your breathing; and I want you to ease into exploring the sounds your voice can make in a way that is completely separated from the ideas of "in tune" and "out of tune" and even "singing." This is why the concrete skills needed for singing are not taught in beginning of the book. However, for some of you, working on these skills might be the most important piece of all. If so, please feel free to skip ahead to chapters 12 - 23.

Why Are Some of the Exercises So Similar?

You may notice a similarity among many of the exercises. For instance, you may be doing almost the same activity in the Self-Assessment section as in the Getting Started section, but you will be doing them from a different perspective and with a different purpose. Much of learning to sing involves repetition (very important when learning music in general) so bring an open mind with you as you proceed. Remember that as you move through the program *you* will be changing, so even similar exercises may feel very different each time you do them. This is a sign of your growth.

Do the Ice Breakers

Sprinkled throughout these pages are "Ice Breakers." The idea is to get you to use your voice right away. When I give a live workshop I always start by getting everyone to just make some noise with their voices. After that, we talk and then later we do more singing. But starting with a noise-making ice breaker dissolves everyone's anxiety right away.

The Ice Breakers in this book serve the same purpose. They are here to get you using your voice in the most relaxed, playful way possible. Don't think much about them – just jump right in and have fun with them!

How to Fit This Into Your Life: Say "Everything Counts"

This is an idea that I've found immensely helpful. As when learning any musical instrument, practicing is crucial, and in chapter 21 we'll discuss ways to successfully build practicing into your life. But early on I hope you can embrace the concept of giving yourself lots of credit for everything you do to make yourself into a better singer. When your perspective is, "everything counts" you will find that building blocks for singing are being created much more frequently and easily than if you only place value on focused and dedicated practice times.

For example: You are in the car and listening to the radio. You notice the singing or the rhythm in a song in a new way. Then you spend a few minutes digesting your new observations. That counts! (Note: I drive and sing, but I'm not advocating this for everybody. Obviously, don't drive and sing if it distracts you from driving well!) If you sing while doing the dishes, that counts. If you're at a party and you find yourself humming along quietly while other people are singing, that counts. **All of it helps you learn, and it all counts.**

The biggest pitfall for my students is not that they don't practice, but rather that they have a narrow definition of practicing that doesn't work for them when it comes to learning to sing in the context of their busy, complicated lives. The students who have been the most successful see many opportunities to practice — even informally.

A Few More Tips

Also say, "Everything Counts" about your successes.
You just read about how to have an "Everything Counts" attitude about practicing. It's also very important to have an "Everything Counts" outlook on your successes.

Appreciate every success as significant. "I actually sang Happy Birthday with everyone else this time at my uncle's party!" "I listened to the song 'Yesterday' and noticed things about it I'd never noticed before." "I was playing around and realized that I can reach higher notes than I thought I could!" "I sang Row Your Boat while I was walking and could really feel the beat in my body!" "I had this insight into why I stopped singing in the first place." "I spent five minutes doing one of the singing exercises." Each one of these small successes counts!

Stick with it.
When the ball drops, pick it up again. Maybe not right away, but when you can. Know that the ball probably will drop but also know that life is long, and look for opportunities to pick the ball up again when life gives you more space. Don't let the idea of learning to sing slip off your radar and disappear completely.

However it works for you to fit this new thing into your life is perfect. Everything you do that relates to singing, even peripherally, counts and deserves acknowledgment. These small successes form the building blocks to larger successes.

Get Ready to Sing! Here's Your First Ice Breaker!

Sing These Shapes...

Follow each of these lines with your voice – whatever interpretation you come up with is fine. You can go to Track 1 to hear my interpretation. You can also draw your own shapes and sing them!

Benefits

Teaches voice control by connecting your visual understanding of high and low with your vocal experience of high and low. Also a great vocal warm up.

Chapter 1
Singing is Your Birthright

So, you have a fear of singing? The first and most basic message for you is this: Everybody deserves to sing! People have been singing for all recorded history — there's plenty of evidence that we humans chanted and sang before we developed spoken language. Singing is a profound way of expressing every emotion, and a great way to have fun with friends and family. We sing as a way of gathering power and energy in war chants, protest songs and sports cheers — and we sing to connect with our sense of reverence and awe. We sing as a way of bonding with each other in community at celebrations, at times of mourning, for relaxation and for the sheer joy of it. We have done so all throughout human history. It is more natural for us as a species to sing than it is to not sing.

Have you ever experienced strong emotions while listening to music? Have you had the feeling that the music was commiserating with your sorrows, energizing your joys, or giving you inspiration when you needed it? Imagine a movie without any music in the soundtrack. That would be quite unusual, since film directors know that music is an extremely effective way to enhance story telling. The power of music to reach in and move us is certainly recognized by marketing experts as well as movie directors, which is why musical jingles are commonly used in commercials. In religious ceremonies, wedding celebrations and funerals, you will often find music playing a vital role. And during everyday activities, such as exercising at the gym, shopping, or riding an elevator, music is often playing in the background, affecting us subliminally.

Take a moment to reflect on how music affects you in your life. Has a song ever made you teary? Have you listened to music to soothe yourself or cheer yourself up? Have you put on music to inspire yourself to exercise? If you are able to recognize the amazing power of music as a listener, then imagine the depth of experience you can have by making your own music, and in particular the expressive and emotional power of using the most primary instrument of all — your own body — to make music. Your voice is a miraculous instrument that you carry around with you every day, all day long!

"And all meet in singing, which braids together the different knowings into a wide and subtle music, the music of living."
– Alison Croggon,
The Naming

Photo courtesy of Ironwolf.net

So to feel that you can't sing, or shouldn't sing or won't sing is a darned shame! You probably have your reasons for feeling the way you do, but life is long and things change. This book is about taking the first step into both a new set of skills and a fresh perspective. I'd love to be working with you in person, in a lesson or a workshop so that we could share our stories and join our voices. This book offers another way I can connect with you and is designed to be as interactive as possible.

The Big Singing Myth: Either You Have It or You Don't

There's an idea out there that with singing "Either you have it or you don't." This attitude drives me crazy. When children have trouble with reading, writing or math we, as a society, have come to recognize that those are essential skills that are ultimately learnable with the right guidance. But with singing, sadly, this often isn't the case. The message "YOU just can't sing" is freely dispensed. Along with: "You will never be able to sing in tune." "You don't have a nice voice." The basic idea is that you should give it up. End of story. Period.

There are cultures where singing is crucial, where everybody can sing — and does sing, as an integral part of life. But in our modern-day world, where we can simply turn on the radio or an iPod to have our musical needs met, participatory singing has been devalued to the point of disregard. We rarely offer so-called non-singers the extra focus and teaching it takes to bring them into the fold.

> **Exercise 1.1: Let's Sing Together!**
> **Tracks 2 & 3 ◀)) Video 1 ▶**
>
> I love to sing, and if I knew you, I'd love to sing with you — yes, *you*! In fact, let's try it right now. Let's break the ice!
>
> Go to the website to find Track 2, where you will hear me singing one long note, and Track 3, where you will hear a male voice singing a lower note. Hum or sing along with both tracks. Don't worry about whether you're getting it "right" or not, just make a sound and enjoy the feeling that the vibration creates inside of you. This is where it all starts — tuning into the beauty of one simple, long note.
>
> That's singing in its simplest form and, congratulations, you just did it!

It takes courage and perseverance to confront and overcome barriers that have developed over time. This is true in any area of life, but with singing the barriers tend to be very personal, profound and visceral. Along with internalizing the message that you don't deserve to sing you also may feel some shame, regret and loss. You may not only think that you shouldn't sing, but that you shouldn't be loud in general, that you shouldn't speak up or speak your mind, that you aren't creative, that you aren't musical, or even that you can't hear properly (as in being tone-deaf).

If any one of these limiting messages (or others not mentioned here) has made its way into your self-concept, then when you take the very brave first steps toward learning to sing, you may be surprised to find that other parts of your life are touched and expanded as well. Along the way you may confront strong feelings of insecurity, self-doubt and frustration, and as you move through and past these barriers, you may be surprised by how empowered, creative and proud you feel. Welcome to the journey!

Photo by Smiley Karst

Photo by Benoît Ferradini / Radio-Canada.
Children singing at Pam's Creche in Esigodini, South Africa.

Photo by Emma Kipp

Some Research About Music, Learning and Brain-Health

Music Making Students Get Higher Marks

"Regardless of socioeconomic background, music-making students get higher marks in standardized tests. An analysis of a U.S. Department of Education database which tracked more than 25,000 students over a period of ten years, students involved in music generally tested higher than those who had no music involvement. The test scores studied were not only standardized tests, such as the SAT, but also in reading proficiency exams. The study also noted that the musicians scored higher, no matter what socioeconomic group was being studied." *Source: Dr. James Catterall, UCLA, 1997.*

Music and Visual Arts Training Improves Students' Attitudes, Behavior and Academic Performance

"In Rhode Island, researchers studied eight public school first grade classes. Half of the classes became 'test arts' groups, receiving ongoing music and visual arts training. In kindergarten, this group had lagged behind in scholastic performance. After seven months, the students were given a standardized test. The 'test arts' group had caught up to their fellow students in reading and surpassed their classmates in math by 22 percent. In the second year of the project, the arts students widened this margin even further. Students were also evaluated on attitude and behavior. Classroom teachers noted improvement in these areas also." *Source: Nature May 23, 1996.*

Music Therapy Treatment Aids Alzheimer's Patients

"We report that music therapy is effective in the treatment of Alzheimer's disease. We found that the secretion of 17β-estradiol and testosterone, hormones that are supposed to have preventive effects on Alzheimer's disease, is significantly increased by music therapy. During the sessions, patients with Alzheimer's disease were allowed to listen to music and songs with verbal contact from the therapist. It was found that problematic behaviors such as poriomania (fugue) had decreased. Music therapy has the potential as an alternative treatment for adverse hormone replacement therapy." *Source: Efficacy of Music Therapy in Treatment for the Patients with Alzheimer's Disease; International Journal of Alzheimer's Disease, Volume 2012, H. Fukui, A. Arai, and K. Toyoshima.*

Chapter 2
Why Sing?

Though I believe in singing for singing's sake, the following pages are here to provide you with any extra inspiration you might need.

Singing Makes You Smarter

There is extensive research showing that practicing a musical instrument, including the voice, helps people learn in other ways as well.

In early childhood, when music is best learned through play, singing helps develop a readiness for speech and cognitive activities in general. With older children and young adults, music learning supports all forms of learning. Research in U.S. schools shows that children who have music training surpass other kids in math, English, and test-taking in general. They get higher SAT scores. As a demographic, children engaged in musical activities also express a more cooperative and enthusiastic attitude in school. Around the world, countries with the highest academic achievement place a high valuation on (and corresponding funding of) extensive music education.

Many experts believe that learning new musical skills reinforces existing neural pathways and helps create new ones. There is evidence that learning music may produce measurable and significant changes in the brain and may help to stave off Alzheimer's disease and dementia. It has also been found to help people who already have these conditions retrieve old memories and to hold onto new ones.

Singing Makes You Healthier

Research shows that in general, people who sing are healthier than people who don't sing. That's probably due to the deep breathing, muscular engagement, stress reduction, and positive feelings that it instills. Because singing involves deep breathing, it engages the whole cardiovascular system, giving the lungs a workout and increasing their capacity. Singing tones the abdominal, intercostal and diaphragmatic muscles and improves posture. When we sing we take in more oxygen, improve aerobic capacity and experience a release of muscle tension, easing aches and pains, and improving mood. Singing boosts

"I would teach children music, physics, and philosophy; but most importantly music, for the patterns in music and all the arts are the keys to learning."
– Plato

Tip

Don't forget that you can jump ahead to Chapter 3 if you want to get started on the exercises now!

"When individuals suffering from Alzheimer's or dementia hear a melody connected with a meaningful memory, they can re-awaken. Many people who have not spoken in years find words and sing lyrics. They often regain the ability to converse and connect to those around them."
– MusicAndMemory.org

Singing...

- *is an endorphin-releasing pain reliever*
- *improves sleep*
- *improves posture*
- *increases lung capacity*
- *clears sinuses and respiratory tubes*
- *tones your facial and stomach muscles*
- *boosts your immune system*
- *increases life expectancy*
- *increases confidence*
- *improves your mood.*
- *releases the same feel-good brain chemicals as sex and chocolate!*

– *"Life-Affirming Benefits of Singing", The Pitch Pipe Magazine, July, 2011.*

the immune system, helping to fight disease and prolonging life expectancy. There's even a theory that the vibrations created in the skull when we sing help to clean out toxins. (I like that one a lot.)

Singing Makes You Happier

Singing releases endorphins and oxytocin into the blood stream and raises their levels in the brain. These feel-good hormones increase feelings of trust and bonding. This science explains why singing is like the best kind of drug, making us feel relaxed and inspired. In addition, singing is a primal form of self-expression. Singing facilitates "letting it all out," in a healthy and enjoyable way, providing relief for stress and depression.

When you sing with other people, you are literally connecting with them on a vibrational level. Your body vibrates (hum a little bit right now — you can feel it in your chest, throat, head and mouth!), the air inside your body vibrates, you cause vibration in the air around you with your sound waves, and the sound waves cause vibration in other people's heads. So as I said, when you sing, you are *literally* connecting with other people through vibration. Once you tune into it, there's no feeling quite like it — it's a real high.

Also, on a more obvious level, when you're part of a singing group such as a chorus, you are gathering regularly to work on a common goal. Or when you are singing around a campfire, or singing Happy Birthday to someone, you are using music to share memories and sentiment. It's a lovely way to get out into the world and share joy with other people.

Singing is Expressive — Sing Your Heart Out!

Often if we don't sing, it's for the same reasons we might not speak up when we wish we could. We are blocked inside by a voice that tells us that we might sound bad, or that we might disturb someone, so we hold back. We may (and it's actually quite likely) have been told explicitly that we shouldn't sing and gotten the feeling that our singing voice is ugly or unworthy.

To allow yourself to sing is to allow your own self-expression and self-acceptance to emerge. You probably listen to music at least occasionally for comfort, for energy, for the joy it gives you, and that's great.

But if you're only listening and not singing yourself, you're depending on someone else to sing your heart out for you, when actually, you deserve the opportunity to do this for yourself sometimes! Again, "let it out, you'll feel better," is a common expression for a reason, and singing fits the bill!

"Cheaper Than Therapy"

What do you sound like? What is your own unique natural voice? What does it feel like to get loud? You may not know yet, but you will, because you're on a journey towards discovering new ways of expressing yourself. Your voice is as personal as your fingerprints, but a lot more relevant to your well-being. Discovering what you have to say, and how you sound and feel when you're saying it, is a way of bringing yourself into the light. What fun this can be! How cathartic it can be! And — as one workshop participant put it — cheaper than therapy!

Singing Makes You Empowered

Well-known writer/physicist Richard Feynman entitled one of his books, *What Do You Care What Other People Think?* An excellent question from a famous independent thinker! Well, actually, we often care way too much. To be empowered is to be able to say, "Hey, I'm going to do this thing I want to do, even if someone else might not like it!" Once you experience this in singing, it's likely to show up in other parts of your life as well. Once you discover your voice you may find it irresistible to express yourself more openly in other settings. Don't say I didn't warn you!

I find that the choice to learn to sing is often accompanied by other breakthroughs as well. I've had students tell me about all kinds of changes in their lives that coincide with the adventure of learning to sing: choosing to go back to school, getting over a divorce and finding a new relationship, getting married, breaking patterns of submission with a parent and finally speaking out, changing careers, losing weight and getting in shape. Without knowing if there is a cause and effect relationship, or which changes came first, I can say for sure that the choice to find one's singing voice is often connected to, frequently supportive of, (and sometimes precipitates) other brave and bold life changes.

"For me, singing sad songs often has a way of healing a situation. It gets the hurt out in the open into the light, out of the darkness."
– Reba McEntire

Singing Makes You Fearless

For some people, taking on singing is a challenge requiring daring and determination. According to research, public speaking is the greatest collective fear of people in the U.S., beating out even death. This means that we are collectively more afraid of being shunned socially than we are of losing our very lives! When people decide that it's time to live a more fearless life, they often imagine taking on death-defying challenges such as bungee-jumping or skydiving. But for many of us, learning to speak or sing in public is at least as challenging as jumping out of a plane. It's a way to face your fears and earn your stripes.

Photo by Matt Herron. Martin Luther King and Coretta Scott King marching and singing with the Abernathy children. Front, Left to Right: Donzaleigh Abernathy, Ralph David Abernathy III, & Juandalynn Abernathy. Left rear (fur hat): Ralph Abernathy.

"The freedom songs are playing a strong and vital role in our struggle. They give the people new courage and a sense of unity. I think they keep alive a faith, a radiant hope, in the future, particularly in our most trying hours."
– Martin Luther King, Jr.

On the other hand, perhaps somewhat ironically, singing can actually *give* us courage in hard times. Take a look at the photos on this page. They are reminders of the important role that singing played in the American Civil Rights movement in the 1950s and 60s.

I remember singing, "We Shall Overcome," with 500,000 other people at the Moratorium to End the War peace march in 1969 in Washington D.C. It was an unforgettably powerful experience for an 11-year-old to join forces with family, friends and thousands of strangers, singing and

Photo by Ted Polumbaum

chanting for a common cause. The music gave voice to our passion and joined us in courageous expression.

I also remember that my first rock climbing experience involved singing. I was wearing all the proper gear, and there was someone I trusted belaying me from the top, but even so I was terrified to be dangling from a rope halfway up a cliff wall. I found myself singing

"Blue Moon" over and over like a mantra that would save my life. Singing calmed me and gave me the boost I needed to keep climbing.

It's interesting to think of using the very thing you're afraid of (singing) to help cure your fear of ... singing; if you can get past your fear enough to get started you may find that the singing itself contains the properties you need to persevere!

Singing Builds Community

Years ago I was part of a large chorus of about 50 women. I was in that chorus from its earliest days and I remember at one of the first rehearsals the director telling us, way before we'd all gotten well-acquainted, that we were a community. This was my first time in a chorus and I remember thinking quite skeptically, "A community? We're just a bunch of women singing together. Just *saying* that we're a community doesn't mean that we actually *are* a community." It seemed to me a corny and somewhat phony thing to say.

Well, it didn't take long for me to discover that I was wrong about that. The director knew what she was talking about from her own experience. Having grown up singing in choruses, she knew about the power of song in creating community. She was kind and supportive; we all made music together each week, and we got to know each other in ways that transcended the chit-chat that is often the MO of other kinds of group interactions. We literally made harmony together; we communed on a different level. And sure enough, many of my good friends now, almost 20 years later, are people I met through that chorus. I continue to find, time and again, that the bonds that form through singing are bonds that tend to be satisfying and lasting.

But perhaps this is not the case for you. Picture this: you're sitting around a campfire, someone pulls out a guitar and people start singing. They're letting loose and sharing songs from the past. If you don't feel comfortable singing, it might not be much fun for you. Rather than experiencing this as a bonding situation, this campfire scene might bring up feelings of inadequacy or even loneliness.

One of the great benefits of getting the support you need, tackling your fear of singing, and learning to sing, is that it will be easier for

Photo by Rowland Scherman.
Joan Baez and Bob Dylan, 1963.

On "We Shall Overcome":
"One cannot describe the vitality and emotion this one song evokes across the Southland. I have heard it sung in great mass meetings with a thousand voices singing as one; I've heard a half-dozen sing it softly behind the bars of the Hinds County prison in Mississippi; I've heard old women singing it on the way to work in Albany, Georgia; I've heard the students singing it as they were being dragged away to jail. It generates power that is indescribable."
– Wyatt T. Walker,
Civil Rights Leader

you to feel part of singing opportunities when they arise. You will feel more confident and relaxed. Instead of watching from the outside you'll be able to be a part of these community building experiences. I think you'll enjoy that.

Singing Is Comforting

As a child I sang a lot (I wasn't "performing" so my stagefright didn't stop me); I know all about finding comfort and calm through singing. I grew up in New York City, where there was always a lot of noise and a feeling of being jostled amid the stimulation. I love New York, but as a full-time resident I needed some sort of buffer. This was before the days of iPods or even the Walkman, so I sang. I sang in the subway, in the echoing lobbies of buildings while waiting for friends, and while walking down the street. Now, as a resident of a small town in New Hampshire, I look back and see that in some ways I wasn't cut out for life in a big city. Singing was my method of emotional regulation. Through singing, I comforted myself and stayed balanced in an environment that was stressful for me. It felt absorbing and soothing. It centered me.

Animaterra Chorus with director, Allison Aldrich Smith. This is the first chorus I ever sang with; I developed many long-lasting friendships that started in this singing community.

We can comfort ourselves with singing as adults, too. Because we can touch deep parts of ourselves with music, and because the vibration of singing is actually a kind of inner massage, singing is very therapeutic and comforting in a deep way. Some people find themselves using their voices in this way without thinking about it. For others it can be useful to recognize singing as a useful tool for creating comfort that you can pull out intentionally whenever you need it.

Singing Calms Children on Long Car Rides and Makes Babies Fall Asleep

Babies comfort themselves through vocalization; they coo and tone with their voices. We comfort and soothe children by singing to them. When our kids got edgy in the car my husband and I would ask them, "How many 'I've been Working on the Railroads' do you think we can sing before we get there?" Sometimes we'd sing that song twenty times. This might not sound like fun to you but it did the trick; it kept them entertained and calm, and we actually enjoyed it!

Every culture has its lullabies; we count on them. When our daughter was little, we sang her to sleep in the car, in her stroller, in her bed and in our arms. I practiced all the songs for my choral performances while putting my daughter to sleep, and she has effortlessly become a terrific singer herself. Sweet memories of singing to her are some of my most precious treasures. Singing to babies and children is a great opportunity to practice with people who are generally not judgemental — although be forewarned, this is not always the case. There are some kids who will tell you to stop, no matter how great you sound!

My son had a whole different relationship to lullabies. He was less interested in the music and the vibe, and more interested in the words. He'd be so distracted by the lyrics of the song I was trying to lull him to sleep with that he'd sit bolt upright and ask me to explain all the words he didn't know. When he was still very little I remember one night explaining the whole plot of the song "John Henry" to him because he wouldn't go to sleep otherwise; instead of falling asleep he learned all about how the railroad industry was changed by the onset of industrialization. If I wanted him to fall asleep to my singing I had keep it to a hum — no lyrics! In other words, if singing lullabies isn't the idyllic experience you were looking for, and even if your child asks you to stop, don't take it personally! They may have reasons of their own that have nothing to do with the quality of your singing.

Singing Creates Cultural Empathy

When you sing a song from another part of the world, from a different time, or about an experience that is very unlike your own, you have the amazing opportunity to tell someone else's story. You are climbing inside their story through their words, melody and rhythms. It's visceral. In a small way, you are experiencing what it is like to be them. When you *feel* yourself into somebody else's situation through singing, it is more than an intellectual exercise; it's physical, it's emotional and it's personal.

In a commencement address at Xavier University, Aug. 11, 2006, President Barack Obama said, "... to see the world through the eyes of those who are different from us — the child who's hungry, the steelworker who's been laid off, the family who lost the entire life they built together when the storm came to town. When you think like this — when you choose to broaden your ambit of concern and empathize with the plight of others, whether they are close friends or distant strangers — it becomes harder not to act, harder not to help."

Photo, Heinz Albers

"Golden slumbers kiss your eyes, Smiles awake you when you rise. Sleep, pretty wantons, do not cry, And I will sing a lullaby: Rock them, rock them, lullaby."
– Thomas Dekker

"Music is the universal language of mankind."
– *Henry Wadsworth Longfellow*

"I think music in itself is healing. It's an explosive expression of humanity. It's something we are all touched by. No matter what culture we're from, everyone loves music."
– *Billy Joel*

Singing is a wonderful way of seeing the world through someone else's eyes. Music is a bridge. In the same way that it's a bridge between parts of ourselves and a bridge to the people around us, it's also a bridge between the very diverse experiences of different lives, cultures and times.

Though I was never good at remembering historic facts and figures that I learned in school or from books, through songs I became fascinated with how other people lived. Singing work songs and spirituals from the American South, Yiddish lullabies, funny American Cowboy songs, British ballads and songs from Balkan villages, songs about mining disasters, love songs, protest songs and rock 'n roll of the 60s, made my world bigger and richer. Singing these songs was like travelling; it was like visiting with people in far-away times and places. Without leaving my hometown I gained a widened sense of human experience and developed curiosity and empathy for people living lives very different from my own. Singing has the power to help us understand each other. Music brings the world closer together and mends differences. In the early 1900s when racial segregation was still the law in the American South, bands were integrating. Musicians for whom it was illegal to sit together in a restaurant or bus, were finding ways to jam, compose and record together. When Benny Goodman hired black pianist Teddy Wilson, the Jim Crow laws were still in effect, but that integrated band became wildly popular despite the general racial climate.

In the 2013 documentary *Muscle Shoals*, Rick Hall, who founded the FAME recording studio in 1959 and recorded such artists as Aretha Franklin and Otis Redding, says, "During that era of recording basically all black acts [backed up by his white studio band] you've got to remember that George Wallace was standing in the schoolhouse door

Left:
Photo by Sukanto Debnath. Village musicians in Hyderabad, India.

Right:
Photo courtesy of Jim and Sam Dowdall. "The Wilingtown Washerwomen" Performing at the Northern California Renaissance Faire.

at the University of Alabama making sure that no black people came to school there."

He discusses, along with several musicians, the unnerving experience of working intimately to make music — whites and blacks together — and then breaking for lunch in a diner across the street where they didn't feel safe or comfortable, just because they were together.

"When I was a young boy," says musician and singer Clarence Carter, "... if I met a white boy, I had to say, 'This is Mr. Robert or Mr. Jimmy'. But in the studio we got away from that. It was Jimmy, it was Robert, it was Clarence. ... You just worked together. You never thought about who was white and who was black. You thought about the common thing and it was the music. ... Music played a big part in changing the thoughts of people, especially in the South, about race. By us being in Muscle Shoals and putting music together I think it went a long way to help people understand that we all were just humans."

The musicians played and sang together, people listened, and it changed the world. Music was an ambassador of cultural empathy.

Singing is Zen

Singing is about as ephemeral as it gets. It's there and then it's gone. The act of making music teaches us to accept impermanence. While impermanence and change can be uncomfortable, it is through finding the ability to live fully in the present moment that our lives become rich and meaningful.

I believe this is why singing is an important part of almost every religion; it brings us into the present moment in a way that puts us in touch with our sense of connection to the universe and our sense of awe. Singing can be very spiritual, and the practice of learning to sing can be a spiritual practice.

Fear No More the Happy Birthday Song

I've spoken with a surprising number of people who dread the moment when the cake comes out and it's time for the "Happy Birthday" song. Actually, this isn't the easiest song in the world to learn. It doesn't start on the root note of the key it's in (more about that later) and it covers quite a range of notes. People often start it so high that when they get

"Music in the soul can be heard by the universe."
– Lao Tzu

Photo by Nancy Salwen.
My daughter Emily's 18th birthday.

"About two weeks into my singing lessons I attended a birthday party, and when the candles on the cake were lit, I jumped right in and led the whole family in singing 'Happy Birthday'! You have no idea what a big step this was for me!"
– Melanie, singing student

to the highest note, it's uncomfortably high even for experienced singers. Often everyone looks towards the Mom, or the person carrying the cake, to start the song whether or not that person is comfortable with singing. People often feel put on the spot. If nothing else, wouldn't it be nice to be relaxed when that cake comes around?

Photo by Steve Evans.
Street musicians of Mazari Sharif, Afghanistan.

Self Reflections
About Chapters 3-7

These chapters provide an opportunity for you to get to know yourself better in relation to singing. You will begin to identify your emotional, cognitive and physical blocks, as well as your areas of confidence and skill.

We'll discuss ways to approach these topics, and do exercises to help you get a clearer sense of your strengths and your areas of vulnerability — which may surprise you by turning out to be your greatest strengths! What we do here will help you to proceed through later chapters and exercises with a clear sense of direction. Understanding where you are now will help you to determine where you want to go and what you should focus on to get there.

For these exercises you'll need at least some of the following:

• A Singing Journal. You can use a notebook and pen, an electronic device, and/or the pages of this book.

• Time (generally between 10 and 40 minutes, although this is flexible).

• Access to recorded music of your choice.

• Privacy.

Tip

Don't forget that you can jump ahead anytime!

Be Flexible and Creative

Be creative about finding times and places that will work for you. Try not to let a lack of an ideal practice situation prevent you from getting started.

Use big chunks of time, stolen snippets of time, regularly scheduled times or spontaneous moments to practice.

Think of your practice like the rain that waters the soil around a tree; even if it's unpredictable, it's what keeps the tree alive and the leaves growing.

Use this book in a way that works for you and your lifestyle.

> *Here's a quick look at what's coming up in Chapters 3-7:*
>
> • What Makes You So Sure You Can't Sing?
> • What Does Fear Mean to You? Breaking it Down.
> • Identifying Your Goals.
> • How Do You Learn? Engaging All Your Learning Styles.
> • Start Where You Are ... Getting to Know Your Skills.

Ice Breaker!
Talking in a Monotone

Stand in front of a mirror and have a conversation with yourself in a monotone. Don't use any of the natural inflection that you use when you speak normally; rather make each word come out on the same note, like an old fashioned computer or a robot. For a short example listen to Track 4. 🔊

You can start with, "Hello. How are you today?" You can try switching pitches with each new sentence, but always use just one note for each sentence.

Next, go find a friend and in a monotone ask them how they are doing. I bet they will answer in a monotone.

Benefits
Teaches pitch control and develops the ability to sustain a single note.

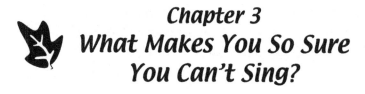

Chapter 3
What Makes You So Sure You Can't Sing?

"My Choral Director Told Me To Mouth the Words."

Most people I meet have a story. This one was my mother's: She was in the 4th grade, happily singing away, relaxed and feeling like part of things, when the director of her school chorus told her that she shouldn't sing but instead "just mouth the words." She repeated this story periodically, and not in spirit of what a bad teacher this was, but rather, "See? I must be a real hopeless case!"

Many people have similar stories, and share them to explain why they don't sing and why it's not worth trying. These stories function as a confirmation of the idea that some folks have it and some folks don't — and that *they* clearly don't! Once this starts, it's very hard to open the door to new possibilities. They've given up, and may even believe that's a healthy thing, though sad. They have accepted it as inevitable in the same way you'd accept that you'll never be a natural blond or never be tall. They take it off their list of things to do or hope for, though it often remains as a hidden, secret wish.

Secret Wish

I find that many people who have given up on themselves as singers, are not at peace with this verdict. On a deep level they still secretly hold on to the wish that they could sing. Unfortunately, when they stopped singing, they stopped getting all the practice and experience that people who do sing are continuing to get. As with any skill, the more you do it the more accessible it is. The less you do it, the less accessible.

The remedy for all this begins with embracing and trusting the idea that with singing, it's never an "either you have it or you don't" situation. We all have it — yes, even you! Some just have more of it, or have easier access to it. For those who don't have lots of obvious aptitude or talent as singers, it's a matter of discovering more about

"Here's how hopeless I am and the reason I know it's true: When I was in high school my music teacher actually reached out and hit me with his baton to make me stop singing!"
– A confession from a neighbor

"I clearly remember the moment I stopped singing; we were in the car. I was in the back seat with my sisters and a family friend, and we were all singing and having a great time. My older sister turned towards me and gave me this look. She didn't even say anything, but her message was so clear. 'Don't sing!' After that I just stopped — I don't sing in front of anyone anymore. I figure that singing just isn't for me."
– Excerpt from a dinner table conversation

"I want to sing like the birds sing, not worrying about who hears or what they think."

— Rumi

"Owning our story can be hard but not nearly as difficult as spending our lives running from it. Embracing our vulnerabilities is risky but not nearly as dangerous as giving up on love and belonging and joy — the experiences that make us the most vulnerable. Only when we are brave enough to explore the darkness will we discover the infinite power of our light."

— Brené Brown

what "it" is, playing with it, discovering who you are in relation to singing, and giving yourself time to experience and to learn. It's more like needing extra help with reading and writing than it is like trying to become a tall person instead of a short one.

Now It's Your Turn!

The following two exercises will help you to put your own story into perspective, a critical step in overcoming your fears. Try to approach these questions with an open mind and with an attitude of kindness towards yourself.

Exercise 3.1: Considering Your Story

Think back on your own story. How did you get the idea that you can't sing, or that you're a bad singer? Or, even if you can sing, that you have reason to fear singing out where other people can hear you? As you reflect, try to identify specific experiences that discouraged you or that you interpreted as a reason to hold back. If you don't remember anything specific, just reflect generally.

Spend a little while writing down any thoughts or feelings about singing that you remember having in the past, along with the feelings that are brought up for you now, as you are writing. Take your time with this, as your insights may not all come right away.

_____
_____
_____
_____
_____
_____
_____
_____
_____
_____
_____
_____
_____
_____
_____
_____

"May the world be kind to you, and may your own thoughts be gentle upon yourself.

May your spirit soar throughout the vast cathedral of your being.

May your mind whirl joyful cartwheels of creativity.

May your heart sing sweet lullabies of timelessness."

– Jonathan Lockwood Huie

Good job! Identifying your negative past experiences with singing can be an effective first step towards interpreting them differently, and giving them less power.

Singing Superheroes

There have been several singing superheroes in my life. They have nurtured me and enriched my life by helping me experience the beauty and power of my own voice. To find your missing singing voice, you may need someone to take your side, to stand up for you. I'm happy to be your singing superhero. Imagine me leaping in (probably wearing a red cape) and saying things like, "Don't listen to *them*! That's only one person's opinion!" or "I wonder why they thought it was okay to say that to you?"

If your discourager was a teacher I might say, "It would have been so much more helpful if they had been more specific!" or "Maybe your teacher had a fight with his wife that morning and he was just feeling grumpy." I would question their authority. I would wonder why they didn't use simple techniques to work with you on improving your singing skills. I would question why they thought that it was appropriate to criticise and dismiss you, rather than give you some support.

While I love encouraging fearful singers, ultimately we need to become our own singing superheroes. One way you can start to do this is by treating yourself as you would a good friend in need.

Exercise 3.2: Becoming Your Own Singing Superhero

Read over what you wrote in Exercise 3.1, and consider what you'd say to support a friend if they told you a story like yours. Write a letter to yourself as if you were encouraging your friend, using the specifics of your own situation. Be comforting and supportive. Remember, this is something important to them — they want to learn to sing — so as a good friend you want to help them to step out and give it a try! Then send the letter to yourself. Wait a few days before reading it, and when you do, allow yourself to absorb the messages. They are from your best friend and singing superhero!

"Singing is a powerful tool for self-realization and for nourishment of others. Developing it is a shared responsibility."
– Meribeth A. Dayme,
Dynamics of the
Singing Voice

Congratulations on Getting Started!

You really can learn to sing. You might not yet believe that, but trust that it's true. I know. I've seen so many "hopeless cases" progress and thrive, and you can too. The first step is to start to understand where your fear comes from, and to begin to champion yourself. Well, you've just done that. Congratulations!

Chapter 4
What Does Fear Mean to You? Breaking it Down

You know that fear is no small thing. And that fear in relation to singing is fundamentally disruptive. It either stops you cold or holds you back from being your most fully present and fantastic self.

Tip

After reading this chapter you might be so in touch with your feelings of fear that you want to go directly to Chapters 8 & 9 to start working on the cure!

Often, we choose to avoid fear rather than to confront it. As with most things, once you take it out of its box, break it down, and figure out which bits and pieces are the most troublesome (and which are just stale old stories), it carries far less power. Exploring your emotions in relation to singing will help you deal with and dismantle your fear rather than continue to be blocked by it.

*"Like all explorers,
we are drawn to discover
what's out there
without knowing yet
if we have the courage
to face it."*
– Pema Chödrön

Often when fear comes rushing in, our fight, flight or freeze reaction takes over and we lose our ability to work with what's going on. I've been in performance situations when suddenly, without warning, I lost myself: I couldn't remember the lyrics to my song or the chords on the guitar. The sensation of my pounding heart replaced any joy I'd been feeling and my connection to the music was lost.

Sometimes the way we experience fear shows up less dramatically. We can recognize some kinds of fear by its symptoms: A slowing down occurs. We observe that we aren't following through on our original intent. Tasks are half finished and goals are stuck, halfway met. We have become passive. Even though we don't *feel* afraid we can deduce that our lack of action is based in fear. We've lost our conviction due to a lack of confidence, or a fear of change, or a fear of disruptive emotions. When this happens our clarity and enthusiasm are replaced with confusion.

When it comes to fear of singing, one or more of these three kinds of fear are usually at work: fear of shame, fear of change, and fear of the strong emotions that sometimes arise while singing. The following exercises are designed to help you break down and identify your own experience with fear. Later, in Chapter 8 we will start working on changing your relationship with your fear of singing.

Photo by Nancy Salwen.
Fear of Singing Workshop.

"Be melting snow.
Wash yourself of yourself."
— Rumi

Fear of Shame & Stage Fright

Embarrassment. Blushing. Heart pounding. Sweating. Shaking. Nausea. These are some of the typical, dreaded symptoms of stage fright. Unfortunately, stage fright is not reserved for performance on a stage. It can happen when singing Happy Birthday at a children's party, when singing in church, or when trying to sing along to a song on the car radio when others are around. You can be overcome with stage fright in the middle of telling a joke to friends. Stage fright is when you feel put on the spot, and the spot is the one place you don't want to be.

You may be afraid of sounding stupid or awkward, of being laughed at or made fun of. You may be afraid of singing out of tune, forgetting the words to your song, or having a voice that people don't like. You might be afraid that someone will say something that will hurt your feelings. And, even if they don't say anything, you might think that they're *thinking* thoughts that might hurt your feelings. This fear is connected to our sense of how other people will react to our voices or abilities. This is a fear of being shamed by other people.

Keep in mind, digging into your fear this way isn't easy! But by doing these exercises you've already proved that you're ready for a change. And this is the time to dig in, overwrite automatic patterns, and create the changes in your life that you want to see.

To better understand your fear of shame, get out your pen and paper and let's get started.

Exercise 4.1: Considering Fear of Shame
Spend 10-20 minutes answering the following questions and write down any random or associated thoughts as they arise.

Envision singing in front of other people. Close your eyes until you have a very vivid image of this in your mind, and then answer the following questions. Who is there? How old are you? What location are you in? What are you singing? Any other specifics?

_____
_____
_____
_____
_____
_____
_____
_____

Staying with this imagined scenario, what do you feel in your body? What physical sensations come up for you? What do you feel in your stomach, hands, shoulders, neck, throat, face? Are you hot? Cold? Does your skin feel prickly or tingly? Do you feel shaky? Scan your body for any tensions you may be feeling.

_____
_____
_____
_____
_____
_____
_____

What emotions are coming to the surface for you? Would you say that anything you're feeling physically or emotionally might reflect a sense of fear? Look for any expressions of fear including tension, shame, discomfort, resistance (can't even get yourself to do this exercise?), dissociation ("I don't feel ANYTHING"). Search now for even mild versions of these expressions of fear. Write down your thoughts.

_____
_____
_____
_____
_____
_____
_____

Photo by Nancy Salwen.
Fear of Singing Workshop.

"When you sing with a group of people, you learn how to subsume yourself into a group consciousness because a capella singing is all about the immersion of the self into the community. That's one of the great feelings — to stop being me for a little while and to become us. That way lies empathy, the great social virtue."
– Brian Eno

*"Practicing an art,
no matter how
well or badly,
is a way to make
your soul grow,
for heaven's sakes.
Now, I mean,
I'm talking about
singing in the shower,
I'm talking about
dancing to the radio,
I'm talking about
writing a poem
to a friend —
a lousy poem."
– Kurt Vonnegut*

You might be hearing a little voice in your head that says: "Forget it, there's no way I'm ever going to sing in front of anybody." "I'm stupid for even trying this." "I sound terrible." And possibly even some version of this: "I not only sound awful, but I look awful too. In fact, I not only sing horribly and look bad, but I'm just generally icky! I have no business asking people to pay attention to me!" Are any of these kinds of thoughts going through your mind? Write about them here.

_____

_____

_____

_____

_____

_____

_____

_____

All of the reflections in this exercise have been about better understanding any feelings of shame you might have around singing.

Now, on a scale of 0 - 10, measure your level of feelings of shame, 0 being, "I felt OK. I don't think feelings of shame are my big issue." and 10 being "This was very embarrassing and uncomfortable." The goal here for you is to identify your feelings of shame so that you can work with them as you proceed.

Level of Feelings of Shame (circle a number)
0   1   2   3   4   5   6   7   8   9   10

Nice work! I know this exercise can sometimes be kind of disturbing.

Because shame so often involves negative self-talk, it can be effectively addressed with positive self-talk. First you acknowledge the thoughts, as you just did, bringing them out into the light. Then you address the thoughts and put them in their place. It's less about banishing these voices than learning to put them into perspective. We'll come back to this and do some work with the fear of shame later. Or you can jump right to Chapter 9 to practice positive self-talk right now.

Fear of Change

I was woken up this morning by the loud grinding sound of trees being cut down in the neighbor's yard. These were big, tall pines that had been there when we bought our house 19 years ago, and that I'm sure had been there for almost a century before that.

Quite a few trees have been removed by neighbors on our block, and I thought that now our street was starting to look bare and stark. Without any warning, I have lost the view out my window that I've come to know and love. Not only am I surprised by the change itself, I am surprised once again by the very existence of change. Trees grow old so slowly that I feel like they are permanent, when of course they aren't. Nothing is. And so my reaction isn't only, "Oh, I'm going to miss those trees," but also, "Damn it, things keep changing. I forgot again!"

My days are full of tasks and errands that shape my life and the life of my family in a way that creates a feeling of order and control, but ultimately everything is temporary and so much is out of my control. The disappearance of that grove of trees, once a fixture in my life, is just today's reminder of that jarring reality.

There is almost always a part of us that fears change. Even if we feel ready to take on something new, be it a new skill or a new way of behaving or thinking in the world, we are usually also afraid of that change, on some level. So when change is in the air, the negative self-talk tends to go into full swing.

This experience is so universal that there are many different words, coming from many different systems of thought, for that voice inside that tries to keep us in our place and stop change from happening. In Buddhism it's called Monkey Mind. It's the chatter, usually negative, that says things like "Forget it, you can't do that." In the world of life-coaching, I've heard it called the Gremlin. "I can't ask her out, she's way out of my league," or "I can't believe I said that, what an idiot," or "Who do you think you are, anyway? Just go home! Give up!" The closer we get to change, the louder and more persistently the Gremlin talks.

When our self-protective subconscious senses a change coming on, it tries to hang on to the familiar, even if it's not all that great. The status quo has become built into our identity, our sense of who we are.

> *"When you open yourself to the continually changing, impermanent, dynamic nature of your own being and of reality, you increase your capacity to love and care about other people and your capacity to not be afraid."*
> — *Pema Chödrön,*
>   *Practicing Peace in*
>   *Times of War*

"Twenty years from now you will be more disappointed by the things you didn't do than by the ones you did. So throw off the bowlines, sail away from the safe harbor. Catch the trade winds in your sails. Explore. Dream."
– (attributed to) Mark Twain

We may not like it, but we are used to it. The move from non-singer to singer is a change of identity. This may be more significant, and therefore more threatening to your Gremlin, than you think.

Our definition of ourself also helps define our relationships. When we make a change, we're sometimes met with resistance from people we're close to. They want to preserve the image of us that they're comfortable with. Have you heard stories about people being offered sweets by their family when they are trying to lose weight, or being offered drinks by their buddies when they're trying to quit drinking? As much as they may love us, people in our lives are not always able to support our efforts to change.

As you start to discover your inner singer, you may find that some of your friends are not quite on-board at first. If you say, "Hey, I've decided to learn to sing," they may joke that you're a hopeless case. Ordinarily you might joke along, but what if you were to change your reaction and say, "No, I'm serious, this is something I really want to do"? Or, can you imagine saying, "I don't actually believe anymore that I'm a hopeless case." Kind of a big deal to say that, right? It might feel as if you're being argumentative, obnoxious, conceited or stupid. And, where will this change lead you? You don't know! Exciting, but scary too.

Exercise 4.2: Considering Fear of Change

For a day (or even for just 2 or 3 hours) notice and write down your self-talk around the subject of change. Are there areas in your life where you're taking on or contemplating something new? This could be a new friendship, a new task at work, a new art project, taking or teaching a new class, or asking someone to marry you. Imagine a scenario in which you're taking the first steps, or telling someone about your intention to take on this change. Imagine the scene and include specific details. Make it feel real.

Notice, and write down whatever self-talk comes up when you are visualizing yourself in activities or conversation relating to these new tasks, or to taking on a new role.

_____

_____

_____

*"The woods
would be quiet
if no bird sang
but the one
that sang best."
– Henry van Dyke*

Now, try this specifically with singing. Out loud, say the words, "I'm going to learn how to sing" and see what kind of response you get from the old Gremlin. Visualize yourself talking to someone in your life and say, again, out loud, "I'm going to learn how to sing." Now how's the Gremlin doing? Louder? Pretend you are saying "I'm learning how to sing" to a person who in the past criticized your singing, or who clearly thought of you as a non-singer. This might be someone in your family, a friend or a music teacher.

How did it go? Again, take notes about any internal dialog that might be happening — what do you imagine that person saying to you in response; what do you find that you're saying to yourself? Were you comfortable stating your intent? Were they supportive? Were you nervous beforehand? If the Gremlin was yakking in your ear, what was he saying? How did you deal with what he was saying? Write about it...

...and, measure on a scale of 0-10 your level of comfort with being different than you're used to being, 0 being "I'm pretty comfortable with this change" and 10 being, "Wow — really uncomfortable with this." The goal here is for you to determine whether a fear of change is a big issue for you.

0   1   2   3   4   5   6   7   8   9   10

"When a problem is disturbing you, don't ask, 'What should I do about it?' Ask, 'What part of me is being disturbed by this?'"
– Michael Singer,
The Untethered Soul: The Journey Beyond Yourself

Just noticing all this inner conversation is great because it's the first step in learning how to talk back, and put those discouraging voices in their place — a place where they don't have so much power over you!

The reality is that change is always happening, every day, but usually not in a way that is as negative or frightening as we fear. You might find that the change created in you by learning to sing is catching, and brings on extra, associated changes, as in, "Boy, I was so sure I couldn't sing, but now I see I can. I wonder what else I can do that I didn't think I could...?" There may be no stopping you after this! You may become more daring and unpredictable, and your life may change.

Note: It is now early afternoon. I keep checking out my window to look at the spot where those trees had been. Now I'm seeing things that those big trees had obscured. The sun is coming into my office differently, there are bushes I hadn't noticed and their leaves are catching the light as they move in the breeze. There is a lovely row of tall pine trees and a maple at the back of the neighbor's yard that I'd never noticed. I'm already getting used to it, and in a way it's nice.

Fear of Strong Emotions That Arise When Singing
Heather was going through a hard time. She had recently divorced and moved to a new part of the country. She was searching for a job and having little luck. She was feeling insecure and vulnerable, but because she'd always wanted to sing, she pushed herself to attend my Fear of Singing workshop, despite her fears.

From time to time throughout the workshop day she'd tear up and cry. The group was kind and supportive, and though she was embarrassed (she was not a person to normally show her emotions this way, she told me) she felt safe and brave enough to stay and participate as best she could. Soon after the workshop we began private lessons, and her emotions continued to be a big part of the picture. Though we focused on skill-building, most importantly for her we also spent time in the place where voice meets emotion. For Heather, this was where much of the value in learning to sing lay; she learned how to use singing as a way of understanding and coping with her strong emotions.

After several lessons, as she was beginning to loosen up, Heather told me, "I never make any noise. I stay quiet. If I let sound come out I have no idea what will happen, or if I'll ever be able to stop." But once we pinpointed that part of her fear of singing was actually a fear of losing control of her feelings, we were able to start working with this.

When, besides singing, do we express emotions vocally? Crying. Yelling. Screaming. Many people are afraid to cry for fear of "losing it." This might mean letting out emotions that feel bigger than you can control. What if you can't stop? What if you get really angry, remember something you've suppressed, hallucinate, go crazy? This may sound overly dramatic, but when you've spent a lifetime keeping quiet, it's scary to think you might open a dam you can't close back up.

I've never seen a student lose control, but I have seen how the fear of this happening has stopped people from opening their mouths and allowing themselves to be surprised by what comes out. And it sure is hard to learn how to sing when you can't let yourself make any sound!

With Heather, I delayed focusing on matching pitch (definition on page 129), practicing songs, phrasing, and other exercises traditionally associated with learning to sing, and spent quite some time guiding her through the basics of simply producing sound, while feeling — with acceptance and kindness — whatever emotions arose. We focused on ways for her to connect with her own deep intuition, so she could express herself naturally through her voice. (You'll find some of the methods and games we used in Chapters 8, 11 and 12.)

It's important to be honest about what you feel in the moment of singing, even when it seems silly or embarrassing. If you're not in touch with what you really feel, you can't access your true, intuitive

"The emotion that can break your heart is sometimes the very one that heals it..."
– Nicholas Sparks,
  At First Sight

self — and that's where all the best gems come from. Singing is an expressive art even if you're singing only one long note. The magic is in the honest expression of who you truly are and how you are feeling as you sing.

"Jesus said, 'If you bring forth that which is within you, what you bring forth will save you. If you do not bring forth what is within you, what you do not bring forth will destroy you.'"
— The Gospel of Thomas

Exercise 4.3: Considering Fear of Strong Emotions

Spend a few minutes responding to this question: "Am I afraid to sing or vocalize because of the feelings that might arise?" Consider: Are you someone who tends to keep your emotions inside? Can music evoke strong emotional reactions in you? Do you tend to experience physical sensations when you are feeling very emotional, such as feeling choked up, crying, tension in your chest or jaw, shortness of breath, etc.?

Exercise 4.4: Fear of Strong Emotions: Testing the Vocal Waters

Make sure you have privacy because you want to feel as uninhibited as possible.

Start by lying on the floor or on a bed so that you can be very comfortable and totally relaxed.

Take a nice deep breath and, keeping your mouth closed, begin to hum, "hmmmmmmmmmm," while exhaling gently through your nose. Stay relaxed. Take a new breath whenever you need to.

Now, begin to pay attention to the physical sensations you're experiencing. Notice the vibrations in your face, throat, chest and stomach. Think of your voice as giving your body an inner massage and allow it to help you to relax even more deeply. Let your mind wander. Make any humming or other sounds you want — you may even find yourself making up a little tune. Feel free to get loud if you want to, or to move around or gesture with your arms and hands. Go with the flow! Give yourself at least five minutes with this exercise so that you have time to see where it takes you.

When you're done, write about how you felt. Consider: Did you enjoy this? Did fear or other emotions rise to the surface? Do you think that vocalizing has the potential to connect you to your emotions? Would you say that there are emotional blockages to your freedom with making vocal sounds?

"My music is so often like a lullaby I write to myself to make sense of things I can't tie together, or things I've lost, or things I'll never have."
– Stephan Jenkins

*"To be fully alive,
fully human,
and completely awake
is to be continually
thrown out of the nest.
...To live is to be willing to die
over and over again."*
*– Pema Chödrön,
When Things Fall Apart:
Heart Advice for
Difficult Times*

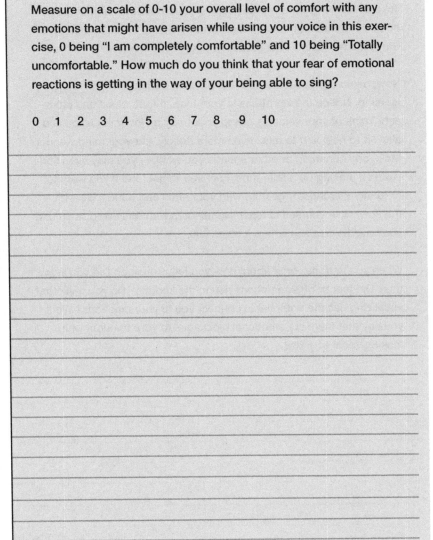

Measure on a scale of 0-10 your overall level of comfort with any emotions that might have arisen while using your voice in this exercise, 0 being "I am completely comfortable" and 10 being "Totally uncomfortable." How much do you think that your fear of emotional reactions is getting in the way of your being able to sing?

0   1   2   3   4   5   6   7   8   9   10

Great work! We'll return to the topic of singing and the emotions in Chapters 8 and 9.

Emotional Connections Can Be Positive!

Whatever you have discovered while going through this chapter is just fine, whether or not your experience was intense, and even if your answers don't seem very revealing. The better you understand your fear and what triggers it, the more equipped you'll be to move beyond it. You can even learn to use fear and other emotions to become a better singer.

Keep in mind that fear is an emotion, and that being in touch with your emotions is helpful for singing. Moving forward, when you listen to a song or watch someone perform, notice how they connect with their feelings as they sing. See how they are moving. Look at their facial expressions, watch their hands. Listen to the emotion in their voice. Notice how their voice changes with the content of their song. Though you may have been powerfully moved by singers over the years, you may not have registered just how much emotion they were putting into their work.

It's this emotional connection that makes singing so rich and so worth it. Yet it may be this very aspect of singing that makes you most afraid. I suggest that you, too, can you give yourself permission to express yourself through singing. You can transform the connection between your emotions and your voice into an asset.

Detours Allowed!

At this point you may want to continue right on to the next chapter which is about determining your goals.

Or, feel free to make a detour and visit Chapters 8 and 9 which are full of suggestions about how to deal with your fear of singing.

On the other hand, if you're getting excited to start singing now, definitely check out the skill building exercises starting with Chapter 10 and start having fun singing right away!

"When we sing, I am one of many, and the individual me evaporates. I am one of 23 university choir members. Not a professor. Not an American. Not a 46-year-old in the midst of 20-somethings. Not a woman trying to outpace the aspects of self she has yet to make peace with. I am simply what we all are — another voice, a set of lungs, some vocal chords and someone who finds joy and comfort in singing"
– Laura Kelly,
  Dispatches from the
  Republic of Otherness

Chapter 5
Identifying Your Goals

Your goals for singing don't have to look like anybody else's goals; what's important is that they be genuine. If you are true to yourself in setting your intention, then you will be able to discover as you go along what work you are willing to do to meet those goals. You may find that you are more easily satisfied than you thought you would be, or that bringing singing into your life is not as challenging as you expected. Or your intentions may shift towards the more ambitious, and you might find that you are looking to take on new and more complex singing challenges because it's so rewarding. Adjust your goals at any time in whatever direction is most appropriate for you.

It's also possible that the word "goal" is antithetical to the approach you want to have; perhaps you simply want to explore, become un-stuck, or free your voice and get far away from goal-oriented think-ing. Once again, there is no right or wrong here — it's all about what is most meaningful to you. Bask in the luxury of knowing that there is no way to get it wrong. As you set your intention, know that it's fine for your goals (or even your relationship to the concept of having goals) to change as you travel down the road of singing self-discovery.

Let the following questions prompt you as you consider what you are looking for from learning to sing. Do any of these sound like you?

- Do you want to feel comfortable singing the Happy Birthday song? Or singing lullabies to your children or grandchildren?

- Do you want to enjoy singing around the campfire or at parties?

- Are you a teacher who wants to be able to sing with students?

- Have you sung in the past but lost your sense of comfort or joy, and want to find it again?

- Do you want to sing karaoke?

- Do you want to join a chorus?

- Do you want to be in a musical?

- Do you want to sing in church, synagog or other religious or spiritual settings?

"Whatever you can do or dream you can, begin it. Boldness has genius, power and magic in it. Begin it now."
– Goethe

"Do not let another day go by where your dedication to other people's opinions is greater than your dedication to your own emotions!"
– Steve Maraboli,
Life, the Truth, and Being Free

- Do you want to be able to write songs?

- Do you already write songs, but want to feel more comfortable singing them?

- Do you want to be in a band?

- Are you already a musician but want to add singing to your list of capabilities?

- Do you care less about singing but want to explore your voice overall, and experience a change that is mostly interior and personal?

- Are you hoping to become more expressive, or more open with your emotions?

- Are you hoping to connect your voice to your body?

- Maybe all you want is to feel comfortable saying "Ohm" in your yoga class.

It can be helpful to measure your progress in relationship to an intention, so that you can be able to say to yourself or to someone else, "When I started I could hardly [whatever your goal is], but now I'm pretty good at that." Or, "Before, I felt scared to open my mouth and let any sound out in front of someone else, but now I sing out loud (in church, with my kids, on camping trips — fill in the blank...) and it feels pretty good!" Goals help to focus us and keep us motivated. If you are attracted to the idea of making measurable progress or if there is something specific that you'd like to be able to do as a singer, then clarifying and defining your goal can be very helpful.

If, on the other hand, your sense of why you want to sing is more about feeling freer or becoming more expressive, you may want to ditch the whole idea of a goal and simply allow yourself to be as present as possible with what you experience as you move through this program and its exercises. Each exercise can be experienced as a meditation, done with an attitude of "there are no mistakes or wrong notes," in which the value of what you're doing is simply that you're doing it in as completely present a way as possible. With this as your guiding principle, the more you enjoy yourself and let go of judgement as you go along, the more you will excel! Your goal, then, is to be immersed and to allow the sound and feeling of your own voice to move you. Don't worry, be happy!

Exercise 5.1: Declaring Positive Guiding Principles

Before declaring your goals, I'd like you to agree to the following guiding principles. They will float your boat and keep you happy as you travel along. They are the wind under your wings, the gas in your engine ... any corny metaphor that works for you! I would like you to connect yourself to this set of attitudes as you proceed through this program. Take a moment now to read these statements out loud. Take a breath after reading each phrase and give yourself time to digest each idea.

- I will congratulate myself for being brave enough to embark on this journey.

- I will be patient with myself and appreciate my progress at whatever pace it comes. Rather than judging myself with harshness, I will approach my progress with each exercise with curiosity and kindness.

- I will connect to the good feelings and sensations that singing and using my voice produces in my body.

- I will appreciate the beauty and gorgeousness that is unique to my voice.

Great! Now write down answers to the following questions:

How did it feel to say those words out loud? Just fine? Awkward? Bogus? Exciting? Whether or not you choose to have a concrete goal, these are your guiding principles. It's a good idea to spend a little time at the outset exploring your relationship with these concepts. They are your home base.

"If you want to accomplish the goals of your life, you have to begin with the spirit."
– Oprah Winfrey

"I can never accomplish what I want – only what I would have wanted had I thought of it beforehand."
– Richard Diebenkorn

Exercise 5.2: Determine Your Goals

In this exercise you will create a list of your goals for singing (or just thoughts about how you'd like to grow). Write down any goals or intentions that come to mind, along with a short description.

Be specific. For example, if your goal is to be able to sing the Happy Birthday song, are you currently at a point where you can't get your voice to sing it at all? Perhaps success for you is just humming along instead of remaining silent. Or, are you able and willing to sing it but not sure that you're on pitch? In this case, your goal might be not simply to sing it, but to sing it in tune. On the other hand, maybe your goal is to become comfortable enough to just joyously belt it out, without worrying much about being in tune. Whatever goals you choose, it will be nice to return to these pages later to see how you've been moving along! Allow room for surprises!

"Success is liking yourself, liking what you do, and liking how you do it."
– Maya Angelou

Down the road, when you look back at this list of goals, you may discover that you have made significant strides and feel satisfaction. You may feel clearer about your goals and know what next steps you want to take. On the other hand, you may find that you no longer feel strongly about the goals you originally chose. I ask you to embrace this paradox: I want you to choose a goal, or several goals now, and then *not* behave in a goal-oriented way as you move forward.

The goal is written down not to anchor you or even necessarily to guide you, but rather to return to at various points as a touchstone; a way to say, "That's who I was then. This is who I am now. I am different now and as I look back at my original goal I can see how far I've come and how I've changed. I have a view of the bigger picture, with my original goal as context, as I consider where I want to go next."

Ice Breaker!

Make a Racket!

It's quite possible that you never intentionally do anything loud.
Singing takes up sound-space in the world, so start getting used to moving those
sound waves around now, by doing something LOUD!

Stomp your feet and say "Boom, Boom, Boom!"
(If you have a young child in your life, pretend you are a giant or an elephant.)

Go into the kitchen and get out some pots, pans, spoons and spatulas.
Check out the variety of (loud) sounds you can make with these "instruments."

Put on some rock and roll music and join the band,
using your kitchen instruments.

Singing in the shower is fun, and so is the bathtub!
(Don't do this one if it bothers you to get water in your ears.)
While you're taking a nice warm bath let your ears sink down
below the water. Try talking, singing and playing around with your voice.
The sounds are changed by going through the water before they
get to your ears — it's pretty cool.

Find a place with great acoustics, and give a whoop!
(Some lobbies and parking garages sound better than concert halls.)

Find a spot with a great echo, perhaps under a bridge,
or on the edge of a lake. Call out "Hey, hey, hey!" or, "Wheeeee!"
Try making lots of different sounds and notice how they are returned to you.
Experiment and see which are the most fun.

Benefits
Provides an
opportunity for
the timid to find
their wild side.

Chapter 6
How Do You Learn?
Engaging All Your Learning Styles

As we discussed in Chapter 2, music helps the brain with a wide range of non-musical functions including math and logic, and generally helps keep the brain fit and agile. Music learning has been shown to open up neural pathways that connect different parts of the brain, promoting all kinds of smarts and health. My own theory, which I see borne out with my students, is that the reverse is also true. Just as music makes us smarter, our smarts — all manner of them — can make us more musical.

How are you smartest? How do you learn best in general? The learning styles that you engage in other parts of your life can be put to use here as well.

Learning Styles are Your Way In

Everybody learns differently. What works best for someone else might not work well for you; this is the core idea behind the theory of learning styles.

Understanding more about how we learn best can help us set ourselves up for success. If we are visual learners, we can create visual cues to help us with our music learning. If we are kinetic or sensory learners we can consciously work with movement to strengthen our sense of rhythm or pitch. Conceptual learners can turn towards basic music theory to understand how the specific song they're working on fits into music theory in general. Auditory learners might benefit from closing their eyes to isolate the element of sound.

With people who are strong interpersonal learners, I find that it's helpful to make eye contact and lean in close while working on pitch matching and singing skills. These people are best able to access their musicality when they feel the close support of another person (if you are an interpersonal learner you might want to do this program with a friend!). Using multiple learning style approaches is like opening all the windows and doors to let the music in.

"That is what learning is. You suddenly understand something you've understood all your life, but in a new way."
– Doris Lessing

Here are some questions and thoughts to help you consider which are your most effective learning styles so that you can put them to use as you learn to sing. Read and write about them here:

Visual — Learning through Seeing:
Do you prefer sitting in the front of the room during classes and workshops so you can get a good view of the teacher, blackboard, and visual materials? When learning something new, do you find clear illustrations, photos or videos to be helpful? Do you tend to talk with your hands, illustrating what you're saying in the air in front of you? Do you find it helpful to take notes or make doodles when you're learning something new? Take a few moments to jot down examples of how you've used visual aids to help you learn.

_____
_____
_____
_____
_____
_____
_____
_____

Auditory — Learning through Sound or Listening:
Do you learn best when listening? Are you sensitive to changes in tone of voice during conversation? Do you like to talk things out? Do you talk out loud to yourself as you work at a task? Do you sometimes find yourself moving your lips while you're reading? If you identify ways in which you are an auditory learner, you can easily align this learning style with learning to sing. Write your thoughts below.

_____
_____
_____
_____
_____
_____
_____
_____

"Learning is always rebellion ... Every bit of new truth discovered is revolutionary to what was believed before."
– Margaret Lee Runbeck

Kinesthetic — Learning through Movement and Touch:
Do you get restless and tense when sitting and concentrating as you're learning something new? Does it help you to get up and move around? Are you good at physical activities that involve repeated motions and muscle memory? (Muscle memory is a big part of learning a song, by the way.) Do you feel as though you don't really *get it* until you've actually *done* it? Jot down a few examples or thoughts about this.

_____

_____

_____

_____

_____

_____

"... don't be afraid to screw up! One of the key issues to learning is making mistakes... if you're not making mistakes, you're probably not having a very good time."
– Robben Ford

Logical — Learning through Understanding and Logic:
Do you learn by classifying, categorizing, and thinking abstractly about patterns, relationships, and numbers? Is it important for you to understand how something works in order to gain a sense of mastery?

Singing can seem mysterious because we can't see the music-making apparatus at work the way we can with a guitar or a piano. When you hear people using certain musical terminology (alto, soprano, harmony, scale, root note, etc.) your preference for cognitive understanding may add to your feeling that music is inaccessible. Does this sound like you? Write your thoughts below.

_____

_____

_____

_____

_____

_____

Please note that even if you never learn this terminology or how to read music, you can still learn to sing. However, if the feeling that you don't know what's going on is an obstacle for you, you'll want to read Chapter 13, to learn some basic music theory as it applies to singing.

"Every act of conscious learning requires the willingness to suffer an injury to one's self-esteem. That is why young children, before they are aware of their own self-importance, learn so easily ..."
– Thomas Szasz

Linguistic — Learning through Language/Words

Do you learn best by reading, writing, listening or speaking? Do you thrive when debating and discussing ideas? Do you do well with written directions? In math class did you prefer word problems? Do you enjoy playing with language (rhyming, crossword puzzles, limericks, tongue twisters, etc.)? Write about it here.

_____

_____

_____

_____

_____

_____

Intrapersonal (Solitary) — Learning Independently

Are you a more productive learner when you're by yourself? Do you feel more free and comfortable to experiment when you're on your own? Do you appreciate the quiet of solitude when absorbing new information? Write your contemplations below.

_____

_____

_____

_____

_____

_____

_____

Interpersonal (Social) — Learning through Social Interaction

Do you learn best when someone else is involved? Do you like to be to be able to ask questions and get immediate feedback? Are you happiest when you're learning in the company of others? In a class? With a tutor? In an apprenticeship setting? Talk about this ...

_____

_____

_____

_____

_____

_____

_____

Later in this chapter we'll look at ways you can use your strongest learning styles to your advantage, but first check out the following two exercises to get even more clues about your unique way of learning.

When it Comes Naturally

My husband tells of going through a period as a young teenager when he became fascinated by tropical fish. He went to the library and took out all the books he could find about them. After several weeks of reading these books, he went to the pet store to buy an aquarium and some fish. When he asked the staff at the store for help, he found to his surprise that, at the age of 14, he knew more about tropical fish than any of the adult staff in the store. This is something he never forgot.

When he wants to learn about something new, he goes to the library and takes out a stack of books. Even now, with the Internet available to him, he's still likely to go to the library and take out that stack of books. He's identified himself as a book learner (referred to here as a Linguistic Learner), and applies this knowledge about how he learns frequently, and with a wide variety of subjects. He is confident that he can learn pretty much anything from books.

"There is nothing more notable in Socrates than that he found time, when he was an old man, to learn music and dancing, and thought it time well spent."
– Michel de Montaigne,
    The Complete Essays

Exercise 6.1: What Comes Easiest?

Name one or two areas where you have expertise. Choose something that you feel confident with but you had to work at to learn (as opposed to "I've always known how to do that"). Examples might be playing tennis, doing mathematics, cooking, playing piano, driving, or working online with social media. Write them down.

_____

_____

_____

_____

When and how did you learn to do this thing? Did you try different methods before achieving mastery? For example, if you chose cooking, did you gain your expertise through using written recipes? Was it important to have photos or diagrams, as well as written words, to refer to? Did you watch cooking shows on TV? Did your parents teach you? Did you have to spend a lot of time cooking before you felt confident, or did having a recipe in front of you give you the confidence you needed right away?

"Then the singing enveloped me. It was furry and resonant, coming from everyone's very heart. There was no sense of performance or judgment, only that the music was breath and food."
– Anne Lamott, Traveling Mercies: Some Thoughts on Faith

When it Comes Less Naturally ... But You Want to do it Anyway!

This is Tricia's story: "I am more of a visual and linguistic learner and prefer to learn through books and images and in conversation with others — I like to write and I speak several languages. I've never considered myself to be athletic, but I wanted to be able to go snowboarding with my son. At first I felt like a hopeless klutz, but I started slow and went up and down the simplest slopes many times. I found that if I played with subtly adjusting my weight from one foot to the other, by moving my hips, I could gain control of the board. It was a little bit like learning a new language, but in my body rather than in my brain. Using this analogy was helpful, since learning languages is pretty easy for me.

"I also tried visualizing a successful run ahead of time and found that when I took the time to close my eyes and imagine myself doing it, it was as if I'd just taken an extra practice run without actually moving my body. After doing that the actual run was usually better. I also spoke the instructions out loud to myself as I was doing them with my body: 'Bend your knees. Lean to the left.' I had to learn new ways of tuning into what was going on with my body, dealing with physical coordination and with my fear of getting hurt, but using these familiar methods gave me something to hold on to. Visualization and repetition, techniques that I was already using in other contexts, were similarly helpful for me when learning this physical skill."

Exercise 6.2: How Have You Mastered Skills That Were Difficult for You?

The goal here is to is discover how you have tackled challenges in the past to reveal learning approaches that work for you. This again is about figuring out how to harness all your most effective tools so that you can use them when you're learning to sing.

Choose a skill you have that *didn't* come easily to you, something you had to work hard at to learn. What made learning this skill difficult for you? How did you overcome those difficulties? What techniques, methods or tricks did you employ? Did you have to learn new ways of thinking or behaving to tackle this skill? Did you have to reach past your comfort zone? Were you able to apply learning techniques from other skills you'd learned previously?

Write about it here...

_____

_____

_____

_____

_____

_____

_____

_____

_____

_____

_____

_____

_____

_____

_____

_____

_____

_____

_____

_____

"A choir is made up of many voices, including yours and mine. If one by one all go silent then all that will be left are the soloists. Don't let a loud few determine the nature of the sound. It makes for poor harmony and diminishes the song."

*– Vera Nazarian,
   The Perpetual Calendar
   of Inspiration*

"Study hard what interests you the most in the most undisciplined, irreverent and original manner possible."
– Richard P. Feynman

Applying Learning Styles to Singing

Most people possess all these learning styles to some degree. What you have just discovered about your own ways of learning will provide you with more options. There are lots of routes in when it comes to learning to sing, and that's great — the more the merrier! For each of these learning styles there are techniques that can be applied to learning to sing, and the more you've got tucked away in your bag of tricks, the more varied and interesting your practicing will be, particularly if you allow your feelings and intuition to be your guide as you choose which techniques to use when.

Visual Learning Strategies:

• Indicate the relationship of the notes you are singing (or aiming for) with hand gestures in the air, or work with someone who can do this for you. (See Video 2.) ▶

• Print out the words to your song and draw lines or marks above or below the words to indicate which notes go up and which go down.

• Sing in front of the mirror and gesture with your hands where the notes of the song rise and dip.

• Clap your hands or tap your foot as you sing, and watch your movements to visually mark the rhythm of your song.

• Refer to written musical notation if you read music, but if you don't, don't let not knowing how to read music hang you up!!!

Auditory Learning Strategies:

• Close your eyes to isolate the experience of the sound so that you can focus on processing what you're hearing.

• Notice any physical sensations as the pitch of your voice changes.

• Cup your hand over your ear so the sound bounces back and you can hear your own voice more clearly. (See page 206 , Video 15.) ▶

• Try singing songs on vocables (la la la, or bum bum bum, for example) to learn the tune separately, before you learn to sing it with the words. It can be overwhelming to learn all the elements of a song at once, and lyrics can be distracting. Singing on vocables instead allows you to focus on just the pure sound of the melody.

• Repetition. Repetition. Repetition. This is great for everyone, but for auditory learners, hearing and singing a song over and over again can be particularly helpful.

Kinesthetic Learning Strategies:

- Stand up and walk around or rock back and forth while singing; the act of moving while you are practicing can help you digest what you are learning more thoroughly.

- Focus on the way the vibration of your voice feels in your body and in the air around you to help you match a pitch.

- Illustrate the story or emotion of your song with physical gestures.

- Stamp, clap or tap, keeping the beat of your song in your body.

- Gesture with your hands to indicate the tune's highs and lows.

- Take frequent breaks to stretch out and release any physical tension.

- Use lots of repetition to build muscle memory.

- Sometimes it's better to think less and just try it! You learn from doing, and after you've done it once, it will be easier next time!

Photo by Tichonov, RIA Novosti.

Logical Learning Strategies:

- Demystify some commonly used musical terminology, such as scale, octave, perfect pitch, major and minor. (See Chapter 13.)

- Learn a little fundamental music theory, and figure out how the song you are currently working on relates to it. (See Chapter 13.)

- Understand the basics of how the voice-producing apparatus works in our bodies. (See Chapter 12.)

- Choose songs with words you understand, or that make sense in the context in which they're being sung.

We ALL learn in MULTIPLE ways, so try as many techniques as you can, and give yourself a large bag of tricks to choose from!

Linguistic Learning Strategies:

- Learn the words of your song first, the way you might learn a poem, before beginning to tackle melody.

- Look to the words of your song for clues about the melody. (For example, which word in your song has the highest note; the lowest; are there groups of words that have the same note, etc.?)

- Write out the words to your song along with your observations. Both the process of writing them and then re-reading them later can be beneficial.

- Talk to your friends about the ideas in this book. Explaining and processing ideas with others can help you understand them better.

- Choose songs with lyrics you find compelling.

Photo by Emma Kipp.

Intrapersonal (Solitary) Learning Strategies:

- Create time alone for practicing.

- Learn to recognize what kind of settings work well for you. You might like practicing in the same place every time, you might prefer to practice outside, or with your dog, or in the shower.

- Honor your practice by designating a private spot where practicing feels special.

Interpersonal (Social) Learning Strategies:

- Find teachers or trusted friends to help you and give you feedback.

- Use call-and-response techniques, imitating the sounds that someone else makes.

- Make eye contact with people when you're singing with them.

- Find group and community singing opportunities.

Everybody

Everybody can benefit from using most of these techniques, and moving among them in an intuitive way, with a sense of curiosity and discovery. Don't feel limited to using only your most familiar learning styles. Try branching out. Maybe in addition to learning to sing you'll learn new ways to learn.

When I was learning to sing, I imitated my favorite singers. I repeated the songs I loved over and over and over, almost obsessively. When opportunities arose I sang with other people. I gravitated towards auditory, kinetic, solitary and social experience to learn. I thought I was probably unable to learn in other ways.

When I chose to become a graphic designer, in my mid-30s, I realized that I was facing a circumstance in which I needed to learn a new set of skills, and that there was no choice other than to teach myself how to do it by reading books. (This was before the Internet.) Whether I liked it or not I was going to have to stretch out into a different learning style and find ways to make it work. I couldn't plunge into a big stack of books the way my husband would; that filled me with too much anxiety. I had to find my own way in.

So I studied only one book at a time, and then focused on just one very small section. I'd often read the directions out loud to myself.

That made it feel more like the hands-on help I preferred and allowed me to absorb the information in a meaningful way, through auditory support. I took a lot of breaks, getting up and moving around, because the activity helped me to focus. That was kinetic support. I chose books that looked approachable, ones with good illustrations and diagrams, which provided visual support. I called other graphic designers so I could have a backup plan whenever possible. So if the book learning didn't work and I got stuck, I had someone to call who could tutor me through a task. That provided social support. This alleviated my anxiety and made it easier for me to focus on learning from the book.

I'd take each new graphic design project, knowing that I'd somehow figure it out on the job. I'd refer to my books and take notes as I went along, and then once I'd mastered that task I could add it to my bag of tricks. (Sometimes it's best to just jump right in and give it a shot — I think we call that experiential learning!)

From that point on, every time I learned a new skill by reading a book, I felt more confident, and the idea that I wasn't a book-learner started to fade away. I learned not only the skills of graphic design, I also opened up to a whole new way of learning — a surprise bonus benefit. These days I'll even crack open a book now and then when I want to learn a new musical skill. We can change and expand how we learn!

The Five Main Take-Aways:

1. There are all kinds of learning styles that you can tap into to learn how to sing.

2. In fact, we all learn in *all* these different ways to some extent, so it's best to have a large bag of tricks and techniques that work with a variety of learning styles that you find effective.

3. If we're observant as we progress, we discover our favorites. If one way doesn't work, then try another!

4. Using diverse techniques that take advantage of multiple learning styles isn't cheating! It's smart, and it's what musicians do!

5. Once you've discovered which techniques work best for you, trust your intuition as you engage your various learning styles when you practice. This keeps it fresh, fun and effective.

"If a man does not keep pace with his companions, perhaps it is because he hears a different drummer. Let him step to the music which he hears, however measured or far away."
– Henry David Thoreau

Photo by Peter Salwen, circa 1996.
My daughter Emily and her cousin William, strutting their stuff.

Chapter 7
Start Where You Are...
Getting to Know Your Skills

When people think they can't sing, they're usually operating from an assumption that singing is one single thing: a single ability that they simply don't have. In fact, singing is a composite of many pieces, including timing, breathing, vocal quality, listening, singing on pitch, moving your body and tuning in to the vibration of your voice. In this chapter we're going to look at some of singing's parts, and begin to discover where you may already have strengths.

Exploring Your Sense of Rhythm

Would you say that you have a strong sense of rhythm? You might be able to answer with a distinct yes or no. Some folks just know they do and it's obvious to them, and others know they have a tough time with rhythm. While doing this exercise, avoid the assumption that rhythm is something you're either good at or bad at. You may not have thought about it, but rhythm is part of your natural makeup, so fundamental that it begins with your heartbeat. We each have one of those and live with its steady rhythm every moment of every day.

"Every artist was first an amateur."
— *Ralph Waldo Emerson*

"Musical training is a more potent instrument than any other, because rhythm and harmony find their way into the inward places of the soul."
— *Plato, The Republic*

As you consider and answer the following questions bear in mind that your goal is to identify what's strong so that you can use it to support what's weak. For instance, if you love to dance but can't tap out a steady beat, then you could bring more movement (dance) into your body when you're singing to help keep the beat. There are more tricks like this you can use once you've identified your rhythm strengths and weaknesses.

Photo by Biswarup Ganguly.
At the Durga Puja Festival in Kolkata, India.

*"Seemed to me
that drumming was
the best way to
get close to God."*
– *Lionel Hampton*

Exercise 7.1: Rhythm

Read the following questions, and circle the number that best applies, with 0 being "piece of cake" and 10 being "very challenging." Then jot down any additional observations or notes.

Are you able to keep a beat in your body when listening to music?

piece of cake   very challenging

0   1   2   3   4   5   6   7   8   9   10

_____

_____

_____

Are you comfortable dancing?

piece of cake   very challenging

0   1   2   3   4   5   6   7   8   9   10

_____

_____

_____

Were you one of those kids who couldn't resist tapping with your pencil or your foot when there was music around? (Are you still one of those kids?)

all the time   never

0   1   2   3   4   5   6   7   8   9   10

_____

_____

_____

When there is no music playing, are you able to tap out a steady rhythmic pattern and sustain it for 60 seconds, or do you find that difficult?

piece of cake   very challenging

0   1   2   3   4   5   6   7   8   9   10

_____

_____

_____

When listening to a familiar song — preferably one you've known since childhood (for me it might be a Beatles song or something by Bob Dylan) are you able to anticipate when a musical element (the beginning of a chorus, an instrumental break, a particular riff or pause) is about to happen? Or are you surprised because that part didn't come in where you thought it would?

piece of cake   very challenging

0   1   2   3   4   5   6   7   8   9   10

"Everything in the universe has a rhythm, everything dances."
– Maya Angelou

Put on some music now and notice the stops and starts, the underlying beats and the accents. Is paying attention to the rhythm of the music enjoyable for you? Is it frustrating? How well do think you understand what's going on?

piece of cake   very challenging

0   1   2   3   4   5   6   7   8   9   10

How would you rate your overall sense of rhythm on a scale of 0-10, 0 being "I feel pretty comfortable with rhythm and keeping a beat," and 10 being "Getting into the rhythm is very difficult for me"? Make a few notes about what you noticed as you went through these exercises. You will be able to return to this section as a resource, finding ways that you can use your rhythm strengths to help you work on your weaker rhythm areas.

piece of cake   very challenging

0   1   2   3   4   5   6   7   8   9   10

So, how did it go? Often people have a stronger inborn sense of rhythm than they do of melody, or vice versa. You may have a hard time keeping a tune but find it fairly easy to keep a beat. If that's the case, then you already possess a skill that is crucial for singing. That sense of rhythm will keep you coming in at the right time and help you to be predictable and solid for people who are accompanying you on an instrument or singing with you. Some say that the most important person in any band is the drummer, because without a strong rhythm, any structured song will fall apart. Music is generally marked out in time, and understanding how to break up that time with rhythm is important. It's the glue that holds a song together. So, enjoy the fact that you already possess a significant building block for singing.

On the other hand, if you found that you didn't give yourself such a high score, fear not! Developing a sense of rhythm, just like the other aspects of learning to sing, is very doable. You just need some guidance and practice. We'll work on this in Chapters 18 and 19.

"When it comes to rhythm, your body is smarter than your mind — trust your body!"
– Nancy Salwen
(Hey, that's me!)

Exploring Your Ability to Match Pitch

Pitch matching is the underlying skill needed for singing in tune. To sing in tune with other people (which is generally what people mean when they talk about being able to sing) you need to be able to sing the same notes they're singing, at the same time. To do that you need to be able to sing what you hear. This is pitch matching.

NOTE ...

Pitch matching is not the same thing as having *perfect pitch*, although many students start off with this misconception. They think that because they don't have perfect pitch that they must be "tone deaf," an expression which, though liberally thrown around, refers to a medical condition which is very rare.

For an explanation of perfect pitch, go to page 129.

Perfect Pitch is unusual and the majority of us don't have it. You do not need it to sing! So if you had this belief, you can just let that one go right now!

Feeling the Notes

What *is* important when learning to sing is developing a sense of what the relationships between different notes *feel* like when you sing them. This is the skill that will help you sing a song or a scale. The very first step is learning to hear a note and, assuming it's within your vocal range, match it with your voice. But here's the tricky bit: How do you know when you've got it right? Maybe you think you're singing on pitch but you're not, or maybe you think you're off but you've got it right.

This lack of knowing creates an opening for fear to rush in! "What if I think I'm doing fine but I'm off? How embarrassing!" You may have an image or memory of trying to sing scales and having your teacher glare at you when you got it wrong, or of being the one person in the group who's messing up a song. The very idea of pitch matching may fill you with insecurity.

Learning and practicing pitch matching can be a truly profound and enjoyable experience, if you can let yourself really feel it. Start simply and slowly with one long note. One long note is a beautiful thing. It's the beginning of the expression of yourself through your voice. You don't need to load it up with all kinds of expectations. You don't need to be a "singer" to create one long note. You don't need to work hard to make your voice beautiful because it's a naturally beautiful thing, full of overtones, humanity and unpretentious expression. When you slow down and let go of preconceptions you will be able to enjoy its beauty and therefore your own beauty — this is your own voice and it's perfect! One long note is where it all begins.

For this next exercise you may need some outside feedback. You might want to work with a trusted, supportive friend who is a somewhat confident singer. This person does not have to be fabulous or professional or advanced in any way; they just need to be able to distinguish when two notes are the same as each other and when two notes are different. It's also essential that he or she will be kind.

There are No Wrong Notes

When you do the next exercise be sure to establish the following ground rule: there is no such thing as a wrong note — we're just gathering in

"When we allow ourselves to be as big and beautiful as we can be, we empower others to rise to their true stature as well."
– James Oshinsky,
  Return to Child;
  The Music For People Guide

"God picks up the reed-flute world and blows. Each note is a need coming through one of us, a passion, a longing-pain. Remember the lips where the wind-breath originated, and let your note be clear. Don't try to end it. Be your note. I'll show you how it's enough. Go up on the roof at night in this city of the soul. Let everyone climb on their roofs and sing their notes! Sing loud!"

– Rumi

formation right now. If you have a helper, tell them that they're not allowed to discourage you in any way. You are not asking them to assess your singing potential or ability. Instead, ask for specific feedback: Am I matching the note I'm hearing? Am I able to correctly assess when I miss a note or when I'm right on? You want specific feedback about what's happening right now. That's it.

If you prefer to work alone, or if no friends are handy, visit the website to find computer-generated resources that will give you feedback on the accuracy of your pitch matching. Feedback coming from an actual person can be more nuanced and encouraging ("You were a little high," "Close but not quite," "You got it!") as opposed to the purely technically accurate feedback of a computer program. I prefer a real person but the computer will do in a pinch.

Exercise 7.2: Unison, Dissonance and Matching Pitch Tracks 5, 6 & 7 🔊

Listen to Track 5: Unison
You will hear an example of two voices singing the exact same note (also called pitch). First you will hear one voice singing for three seconds and then it will be joined by another voice singing the same note. This is called "unison." Play this a few times to get a feel for what unison singing sounds and feels like. At the end of the track you'll hear unison singing with a male voice and with mixed male and female voices. It's generally easiest to sing in unison with a voice of your own gender.

Next, listen to Track 6: Dissonance
You will hear the first note sung alone for three seconds and then it will be joined by another note that is very close but not the same. This is called "dissonance." Play this a few times to get a feel for what dissonance sounds and feels like. Listen to the end of the track to hear dissonant singing with a male voice and with mixed male and female voices.

I think of unison as creating a smooth feeling while dissonance creates more of a choppy feeling. Notice and compare these sensations. I enjoy them both!

Now it's your turn. Track 7: Matching Pitch

You'll hear a variety of pitches: First female, then male. You will be listening and singing along. Now that you have a sense of the difference between unison and dissonance, try to both listen to and *feel* what is happening as you try to match the notes with your own voice.

Are you able to sing in unison with what you're hearing? Your answer will either be "yes," "no," or "I can't tell." If you can't tell, you'll need a friend to help you with this exercise. Ask them to let you know if they think you're matching the notes on Track 7. (If you're working alone, go to the website and follow the links to the pitch-matching resources there.)

If you are working with a friend, here's something else to try. Ask your friend to sing some notes for you to try matching. Sit close together in facing chairs and have them sing a note for you; one long note on a full breath. They will drone out the note long and steady and you will try to match it. Ask them for feedback. Try it a few times (it may take some practice for your friend to be able to hold their note and give you feedback at the same time). Then try it with a different note. Give yourself plenty of time to try this. Stick with it for at least five or 10 minutes, using a variety of different notes covering a wide range of pitches, from notes that are quite low to ones that are quite high.

How did that go? Let's start by thinking and writing about what this experience was like for you ... anything you noticed (was it easier with high notes, low notes, when you sat closer, when you made eye contact, etc.), including any emotional reactions.

"And all meet in singing, which braids together the different knowings into a wide and subtle music, the music of living."
– Alison Croggon, The Naming

Photo by Robert R. Leahey. Members of Carver School playing a singing game called "Zoodio Zoodio" at the Florida Folk Festival, White Springs, Florida, May 1959.

Now, circle the number that best describes your ability to *know* if you're matching a pitch (regardless of whether or not you are able to actually match a pitch) with 0 being "I can tell when I'm matching a pitch and when I'm not," and 10 being "I can't tell at all when I'm matching a pitch or not."

I know									I can't tell	
0	1	2	3	4	5	6	7	8	9	10

As best you can, try rating your ability to match a pitch — your ability to actually sing the same note as the one you're hearing. Use 0 for "I have no problem at all singing the note that I'm hearing," and 10 for "It's impossible for me to sing a note that I'm hearing."

I can									I can't	
0	1	2	3	4	5	6	7	8	9	10

Write a little more about how all this feels to you. This might be kind of loaded — working with your ability or difficulty with matching pitch can be emotional.

_____

_____

_____

_____

_____

_____

_____

_____

_____

_____

Remember to be non-judgemental here. If you find it difficult to match a pitch, you are not alone and not hopeless! With supportive feedback and practice, you can learn to keep pitch and carry a tune. Don't let anyone tell you different!

If you want to work on pitch-matching right now, you can jump to Chapter 14, "Matching Pitch and Singing with a Drone Note," or continue on to the next chapter, "What To Do About Your Fear?"

Getting Started
About Chapters 8 - 12

Learning to deal with your fear and emotions around singing, supporting your voice with your breath and diaphragmatic muscles, connecting your voice to your whole body, and deep listening, are all skills I work on with students during workshops and lessons. In Chapters 8-12 we'll be using these proven techniques to help you explore your own sound and find your voice.

You can either work through these chapters in order, or pick and choose the chapters that feel most important to you.

It's hard to sing when you can't make any noise!

So, relax and learn to explore, play, and make friends with your voice

Although there is no one right order, I tend to begin with this exploring approach before settling down to focus on developing skills such as pitch matching and rhythm.

Ultimately, your practice will probably consist of a fluid combination of many of these different exercises. You will learn to move back and forth intuitively between activities that are sensory, spontaneous, expressive and free, and activities that are focused and analytical, in which you will compare, contrast and self-correct.

This is not unusual; even experienced professional musicians tend to move back and forth between playing or singing in a way that feels loose and perhaps improvisational, and the more rigorous practicing of specific skills.

When you are ready to begin developing your own practice, an important component will be warming up. Many of the exercises in this "Getting Started" section make great warm-ups that you can incorporate into your practice later.

In Chapters 20 and 21 we'll cover more about structuring your warm-up and practice sessions.

Here's a quick look at the lessons coming up in Chapters 8-12:

- What to Do About Your Fear
- More Fear-Busting Techniques: Transcending Negative Self-Talk
- The Singing Body Connection
- Listening for Singing
- Anatomy and Breathing

Ice Breaker!

Sing a Lullaby

You can begin this activity with a song or with random sounds.
If you already know a simple song or lullaby you might start there.
Or start by making any sound that feels good to you –
maybe an "oooh" sound or a hum.
Imagine that you are putting someone to sleep with your voice.
Sing to a child, a cat, a pillow, or to yourself.
See how quiet and gentle your voice can be.
Notice and enjoy the soothing quality of the vibration
of your voice in your chest, throat and face.

Benefits

Acquaints you with the
subtler side of your voice,
and allows you to develop
more sensitivity.
Builds awareness of the
feeling, as well as the
sound, of your voice.

Chapter 8
What to Do About Your Fear?

Here's what it all boils down to:
Love > Fear
Love is greater than fear.

By love, I mean a deep acceptance and appreciation of yourself in all your imperfection. I mean the feeling of being swept up by a beautiful tune or a powerful lyric. It's the unselfish, benevolent care you sometimes feel for the important people in your life. It's the sentimental part of yourself that cries in the movies. By love I mean the feeling of being connected to all that is good.

Love > Fear is something you practice, over and over:
You talk to the fear.
You remind yourself that love > fear.
You ignore the fear — you let yourself forget about it!
You remember what you are afraid of, and ask, "Is it *still* that scary?"
You answer the question by saying, "love > fear."
You talk to other people about feelings of shame and fear.
You share the idea that empathy > shame, and love > fear.
You sing a song about fear and courage.
You feel the fear and listen to how it makes your voice shake.
You sink into the knowledge that love > fear, and sing anyway.

By practicing love > fear, the fear gets smaller, the love gets bigger, and you have more and more fun!

I'm speaking literally. This is what you do. This is hands down the most important thing I have to share, and everything else we do to deal with fear is ultimately about how to get yourself to a place where you are able to feel love. Why are you doing this anyway, if not for love? Love of yourself, love of the song you are singing, love of music, love of life, and ideally, the new love of your own uniquely gorgeous voice. In love you will find the self-compassion and inspiration you need to carry on through and past fear and on into the music.

"So many people are shut up tight inside themselves like boxes, yet they would open up, unfolding quite wonderfully, if only you were interested in them."
– Sylvia Plath

Photo, Library of Congress, Van Vechten Collection. Portrait of Harry Belafonte, singing, February 18, 1954.

The Embodied Voice Sounds Like It Really Feels

Here's an interesting thing...

It took me a while to realize the extent to which the singers I like listening to are expressing emotion when they sing. They are emoting big time! They are being honest and expressing themselves with conviction — they are not holding back. This is what I mean by love; they are *all in*. Sometimes they're actually screaming, or pleading. Sometimes they are quiet, almost whispering. They are telling a story that truly interests them. And they are telling it in a way that only they can tell it.

In the next exercises you're going to listen to a lot of music, and you'll be making observations and asking yourself questions as you listen.

Exercise 8.1: Listening for Emotion and Variety in the Singers' Voices

On the next few pages you'll see a list of songs and their singers, divided into four groups. Listen to at least one or two recordings from each group (you can probably find these recordings online). By choosing artists from each of these lists, you're bound to hear a wide variety of vocal styles. You can find links to many of these songs on the Fear of Singing website.

Notice how different each singer's voice is, and how that's a good thing! Some are rough and gravelly, some are lyrical and lovely. But no voice is better than another. As listeners we're not objective; our preferences are very personal.

For example, compare Tom Waits to Dolly Parton. Compare Pavarotti to Blondie. You may have an idea of what you feel constitutes a good singing voice, but is there such a thing? These singers take the voices they have and they run and delve and soar with them. They put love into their singing. They sink into their songs and push the limits — and you can do that too. The magic is in discovering our own voices and learning what we have to work with, and then working with it. And learning to love it. Maybe not in that order.

Below the list of songs, you'll see comments and questions. Read these, and while you're listening write about your thoughts and reactions.

SHOW TUNES AND OPERA

Show Me (from My Fair Lady), sung by Julie Andrews

Get Me To The Church on Time (from My Fair Lady), sung by Stanley Holloway

The Impossible Dream (from Man of La Mancha), sung by Joan Diener & Richard Kiley

Aldonza (from Man of La Mancha), sung by Joan Diener

Tonight (from West Side Story), sung by Marni Nixon and Jim Bryant

Nessun Dorma, (from Turandot), sung by Pavarotti

Oh What a Beautiful Morning (from Oklahoma), sung by Gordon MacRae

Cheek to Cheek (from Top Hat), sung by Fred Astair and Ginger Rogers

Singing in the Rain (from Singing in the Rain), sung by Gene Kelly

Adelaid's Lament (from Guys and Dolls), sung by Faith Prince

The Way We Were (from The Way We Were), sung by Barbara Striesdand

Stormy Weather (from Stormy Weather), sung by Lena Horne

DUETS

In Spite of Ourselves, sung by John Prine & Iris DeMent

The Girl from Ipanema, sung by Astrud Gilberto & João Gilberto

All the Road Running, sung by Mark Knopfler & Emmylou Harris

Stormy Monday, sung by Dianne Reeves & David Peaston

FEMALE SINGERS, VARIOUS GENRES

One Way Or Another, Blondie

Strange Fruit, Billie Holiday

Angel From Montgomery, Bonnie Raitt

The Christians and the Pagans, Dar Williams

Bring Me Little Water, Sylvie, Sweet Honey in the Rock

In the Still of the Night, Ella Fitzgerald

Midnight at the Oasis, Maria Muldaur

Jolene, Dolly Parton

La Vie En Rose, Edith Piaf

I Can't Stand the Rain, Anne Peebles

Rock Me (In The Cradle Of Love), Deborah Allen

Baya Jabula, Miriam Makeba

Hotter Than Mojave In my Heart, Iris Dement

Me and Bobby McGee, Janis Joplin

East Virginia, Joan Baez

Sto Morava Mutna Tece, Traditional Serbian

Someone Like You, or, Make You Feel My Love, Adelle

R-E-S-P-E-C-T, Aretha Franklin

Crazy, Patsy Cline

Rock Me, Sister Rosetta Tharp

> "When I first heard Elvis' voice, I knew that I wasn't going to work for anybody ... hearing him for the first time was like busting out of jail!"
> -Bob Dylan

> "I'm on fire when I sing, I'm completely in character, I use my sense memories, and every syllable of it is meant. It's a very special thing."
> – Sinead O'Connor

MALE SINGERS, VARIOUS GENRES

Girl From the North Country, Joe Cocker and Leon Russell

Don't Think Twice, It's All Right, Bob Dylan

Ebb Tide, Frank Sinatra

As Time Goes By, Dooley Wilson

What a Wonderful World, Louis Armstrong

It's Just a Matter of Time, Randy Travis

Maacina Tooro, Baaba Maal & Mansour Seck

You Got to Walk That Lonesome Valley, Mississippi John Hurt

Songs using Tuvan Throat Singing, performed by Huun-Huur

When a Man Loves a Woman, by Percy Sledge

I Believe (When I Fall in Love it Will be Forever), by Stevie Wonder

The Band Played Waltzing Matilda, The Pogues

Camil, Graham Nash

Friend of the Devil, The Grateful Dead

Life During Wartime, or, Psycho Killer, Talking Heads

Night Train to Memphis, Roy Acuff

Mustang Sally, The Commitments

Morning Has Broken, Cat Stevens

Java Jive, The Ink Spots

Uncle Harry, Noel Coward

Any thoughts? Observations? What do you notice as you listen? Which songs and singers move you the most and why?

Notice how each singer is telling a story or painting a picture with their song. I'll bet that with any of the songs you're hearing you're not just enjoying the song because the singer has a nice voice; if they were just singing to show off their fabulous voices, their songs wouldn't move us. What makes these songs powerful is that the singers are expressing genuine emotion. Because they themselves are moved, we also feel moved. The song has power because the singer is using their voice in the service of the song. They are connecting to and channeling its message.

We may not remember the tune or understand all the words, but the feeling of each singer comes through loud and clear and sticks with us even after the song is over. When Aretha Franklin sings "R-E-S-P-E-C-T," we know just what she's talking about, right?! She's feeling it!

As you to listen to these musicians, absorb a sense of what it means to "sing well," and just how wide a range that description covers. We hear a lot of different emotions in these songs — yearning, anticipation, exaltation, passion, grief, anger and bliss, to name a few. We hear a wide variety of voices singing in a wide variety of styles. Is there really any such thing as a "bad" voice? I would say no. There are as many voices as there are people. What's key is to discover everything you can about *your* unique voice and what it can do.

There is more richness in each voice than you may realize. Understand that there is a place for you in the world of singing.

To sing with conviction, a singer needs to pick songs that have meaning to them. What are some songs that have meaning to you, that move you or interest you? What types of songs would you like to sing? If you are coming up blank, talk to friends or browse the internet to get ideas. What songs have the potential to make you feel the love?

List 10 or more songs you are interested in singing. Bear in mind that some songs on your list may be too difficult for you to learn right away, but it's great to have them written down here as goals and to inspire you. In addition, write down what interests you about the songs you've picked, and in what context you've heard them sung in the past, along with any other thoughts or observations you have about them.

SONG: YOUR OBSERVATIONS:

SONG:	YOUR OBSERVATIONS:

Any more thoughts? Observations?

As we go through the skill-building exercises later in this program, try to stay connected with the simple truth of who you are in each moment. Even if all you're doing is singing one long note, see if you can be connected to your genuine self, and let that connection be the cure to your fear.

Finding YOUR Voice

You don't have to sound like anyone else. You don't have to put on airs or affectations. Start simple. Find out what's there and see what happens. Every voice has something special about it, just the way every person does. There is something special and beautiful about *your* voice. Be yourself, and have as loving, curious, and accepting an attitude about who you are and how you sound, as you possibly can. That is the key. Choose to move towards your feelings of love for music, of the sound you're making, of the sensations you're feeling and of yourself. Focusing on love helps you to step a little further away from your fear so that it starts to lose its power. Remember, Love > Fear.

Techniques to Help You Move from Fear to Love

First, Recognize Fear as a Feeling

Because fear often produces physical symptoms and negative thoughts, it is very convincing. Fear is designed by evolution to feel real and important so that we are geared up to deal with whatever danger is imminent. In the case of singing, fear has the power to persuade us to stop before we even get started, although we're not in real danger.

If your voice is shaking or you feel that you're not singing in tune, you might very well choose to stop and find something more comfortable to do instead. Fear might make you muddle-headed so that you can't remember the words of the song you're singing or how the tune goes. Fear can make you feel sick or nauseated. Your fear may barrage you with reasons why you can't sing. None of this is pleasant or encouraging. But we can respond to fear differently when we remember that it's not communicating wisdom to us; fear's words are not truths. Fear is just a feeling.

Photo permission from Wikipedia Commons. An American service-womam teaches a group of girls a clapping game. Jakarta, Indonesia, 2012.

When you recognize that fear is just a feeling, you don't have to let it get in the way of your choices. Know that it will fade and dissipate, just like all feelings do, and don't let it stop you. In time and with experience, singing will become less scary for you, and be more rewarding and fun.

Let Your Fear Help You to Reach Your Other Feelings

Recognize that fear is a feeling loaded with the potential to help you. Fear is an emotion that is made of many emotions — and as we just discussed, singing is all about emotion. If you had the chance to sing while you were feeling afraid and your voice was shaking and you could hardly think, what would your song be? If you could sing while sticking with that feeling of fear, what other emotions might emerge? Would you be singing a song of sadness or of loss? Of love, beauty, and your own gloriousness? Would you cry? Would you howl? Would you crow?

Fear rises to the surface because it has a job. Fear's job is to stop us, so it pops up first to bar the way to further action. All these other emotions that are so near the surface are being held back by the fear. The fear keeps us well-behaved and quiet. Fear acts as an inhibitor. In the same way that the feeling of pain inhibits us from putting our hand in the fire, the feeling of fear keeps us from connecting our emotions to our voice. Because if we sing out who knows what we might feel? It might be something painful or surprising. We might remember something we've forgotten. We might cry or make fools of ourselves.

In this way, our fear is trying to do us a kindness, by protecting us from trying something risky. Fear doesn't want us to feel uncomfortable or get hurt. If you acknowledge the fear and think of it as a door to what lies just underneath it, you may discover the emotions, stories and compassion that will fuel your singing and make it richer and more honest than it would have been otherwise.

Do It Anyway

Fear can stop us from doing wonderful things and cause us to narrow our horizons. If you've let fear hold you back from singing, it might just be time to feel the fear and do it anyway. After all, no one's *really* going to get hurt. You won't kill anyone. You won't wipe out your life's savings. Your loved ones won't abandon you. The worst that can happen is that you will feel uncomfortable.

As we explored in Chapter 4, fear is a general term, and can be made up of any number of components, which can be expressed through a wide variety of symptoms. The simplest scenario is that you will feel nervous while you are singing at first, and you can simply regard that as part of your practice. If your voice is shaking, then let it shake! Experiment with a different sound or song and see if it still shakes or if it lets up a little bit. Check it out. You need to get used to this brand of nervousness so that it's not such a big deal and doesn't keep you from concentrating on what you're trying to learn and explore. What a good thing to be able to do! How useful this is for us all, in any area of our lives! Don't let the fear be a barrier, but instead feel it, move through it, and allow it to diminish. It will diminish and you will become free to learn how to sing!

The more complicated scenario is that you may feel more than just nervous. You may be confronted by feelings of extreme shame or self-doubt. If you can give voice to the fear and openly see what evolves and what other emotions arise, you are into some rich territory! This is where you can begin to tap into the transformative power of singing. Even if the only sound you make is a hum, you are now beginning to make that connection with your authentic, expressive voice. This is also a time when there's a lot to be gained by writing about what is coming up for you.

Tune Into Physical Sensation

Singing creates really nice sensations in the body. The vibrations created by your voice can be felt in your chest, throat and face. Another way to deal with fear is to ground yourself by turning your attention to how it feels physically when you sing. We'll work a lot with this in Chapter 10 but for now you can consider the following:

• When you are nervous it helps to focus on the feeling of your breath coming into your body as you inhale; this puts you into a calmer and more meditative state.

• As you exhale, notice all the places where you can feel the vibrations of your voice — it's a very good feeling!

• Notice the weight of your body and the solid connection of your feet to the ground, or your butt to your chair. Tune into the ways your weight is being supported.

Embarrassment vs. Shame

Author Brené Brown, Ph.D. has done some excellent work on shame that is relevant here. In her audiobook, *Men, Women, and Worthiness: The Experience of Shame and the Power of Being Enough*, she talks about the difference between shame and embarrassment. She defines shame as a feeling of being deeply and fundamentally bad, unworthy of connection, flawed, etc. She defines it as being crucially different from embarrassment, because with shame, you have totally bought in. "I am unworthy. I am stupid. I am ugly. I am a terrible singer who doesn't deserve to make a sound. I am a fool because I thought I sounded good, but then they told me I didn't."

With embarrassment, on the other hand, there is a part of you that knows that the experience of embarrassment isn't permanent, that it doesn't reflect that you are fundamentally flawed, that you are not alone in the world with this feeling, and that everyone feels embarrassment sometimes. Brown works with techniques that help transform the experience of shame into something that can be moved through and past so that instead of having life-blocking, growth-blocking shame, we have uncomfortable, but passing, embarrassment.

What she says about shame and embarrassment can be applied beautifully to the process of learning how to sing. Many people who wish they could sing, but have had life experiences that convinced them they can't, may feel blocked by extreme shame in connection with singing. If this sounds like you I suggest you check out Brown's extensive work on what she calls "shame resilience."

From Singing to Feeling and Back Again

The next exercises are designed to help you approach the place in yourself where singing meets emotion, from two opposite angles. The first one takes you to emotion through vocalization, and the second is the reverse; it will help you get to vocalization by starting with emotion. Both of these will help you develop a new relationship with singing — one that is less filled with fear.

Exercise 8.2: From Singing to Feeling

Pick a song or a piece of music that you find particularly moving or evocative. Find a place where you have plenty of privacy and will be comfortable making some noise. Put on the music and close your eyes. Let your feelings rise to the surface. Breathe deeply and let any images and associations become stronger. Without worrying about whether you're singing correctly or on key, start to hum or sing along. Move to the music if that helps you get in the mood, or even pretend that you're holding a microphone and performing the song, or that you're singing it to someone else.

Go for it, ham it up! Exaggerate. Do you find that your feelings are getting stronger? This can be a little bit like writing in a journal. As you are delving, you may discover new things about yourself, make connections or find your emotions flowing in unexpected ways. As this happens, just keep making noise. Keep your emotional experience connected to your voice. What emerges might sound like singing to you or it might not. During this exercise, your job is not to make that judgement, but rather to push the boundaries of vocal expression and discover what this feels like.

When you're done, spend a little time writing about the experience.

From Feeling to Singing

Courtney had just finished graduate school and moved back in with her parents. At our first lesson she explained that when she was little she loved to sing, but then something changed. When she was in grade school she told her mother that she wanted to join the school chorus and her mom responded by *laughing* at her. Courtney's interpretation (not surprisingly) was that she was so awful that the mere thought of taking singing seriously was hilarious. She gave up, but felt the loss. So how brave was it for Courtney to start taking singing lessons now? Extremely brave!

She had a lot going on: She was challenging old ideas about herself and opening up through her voice at a transitional and difficult time in her life. Her feelings and insecurities were at the surface; she was nervous! I'm not sure if she'd have said that lessons were exactly *fun* for her in the beginning, but she clearly felt that she'd touched on something important.

During our subsequent lessons we worked on pitch matching using techniques I share with you in this book including drones, slides and improvisation. We also worked on simple songs. Her skills improved but what was especially powerful was how she began to connect her voice to what she was feeling. She once told me as she walked in the door that she didn't know if she could sing today — everything was going wrong. She felt too down and too upset to sing. She was exhausted. I suggested we lie down on the rug and just talk and make sounds; we would play with whatever emerged. Intuitively, we found our way into what became the next exercise.

Courtney began to put sound to her feelings, with me joining in as her backup band. We made some pretty crazy noise together and when she was done she stood up, and the first thing she said was, "Wow, that was fun — kinda crazy, but fun!" She felt much better and when we moved on with the lesson, she sang much more freely and accurately. Once she got more comfortable vocally expressing her emotions there was a sense of having cleared away some debris; she could listen, focus, and feel physically what her voice was doing much more clearly.

Exercise 8.3 Preamble
I recommend doing this next exercise in privacy, because it involves a completely uncensored spewing of thoughts and emotions of any sort that arise; a luxury that we don't typically have so long as we are even minimally well-behaved members of society. It's rare that you can say anything you want, in any crazy way you want to say it!

Ordinarily, we're somewhat careful not to hurt people's feelings; we resist the impulse to whine and complain. We don't want to get in trouble or be fired from our jobs because we're hurling insults at the boss. We don't want to say cruel things that we don't really mean to people we love. But sometimes it's good to just let-her-rip, and this exercise provides one of those opportunities. It's part of your singing program. You have permission.

Even if you don't have anything very intense to spew, remember, there is a purpose to this exercise. It will help you connect your emotions to your voice, so that you can become more open and expressive vocally, and start busting through your fear of singing.

There are also other bonus benefits to doing this. Much like journal writing, this exercise can help you to clarify what's bothering you. It can also be very funny. You might find that you're comforted or amused right out of your bad mood. Give it a try and be surprised! And all the while you will be making that connection between your feelings and your voice, which is so important for singing.

Exercise 8.3: From Feeling to Singing

1. Find yourself a private place. An empty house, a spot out in the woods, or inside a parked car (don't do this while driving!) are perfect places.
2. Have a box of tissues handy.
3. Be set up for writing afterwards

Choose a time when you're feeling strongly about something. You can do this when you're feeling great, but you also want to be sure to try it when you're upset. I will work here with a scenario of your being angry, hurt or sad. If you are doing this in a happy mood, you can substitute the type of phrases I suggest with happy phrases. Whatever fits your mood — you're the boss.

Start by complaining or stating how you feel in words, out loud. So, for example you might say, out loud, "I'm so sad, I'm so sad." Or you might say, "I hate him, he's a jerk," or even "Nobody loves me," or "I can't believe I broke that vase — she's gonna kill me." Just say what's on your mind, however silly or petty it sounds, out loud. Wallow in self-pity if that's where you're at.

Start by finding a little phrase that rings true and repeating it a few times. Next, sing it. Make up your own little tune. If it's hard for you to make the jump from talking to singing, start by singing the words on a monotone (all one note) a few times, and then sing one word higher or lower than the other notes. This will force the change from talking to singing and will jump start your little song.

Your song doesn't have to conform to any standards. It doesn't have to be pretty, have any consistent rhythm, or have any kind of form. Let one thing lead to the next. Have no worries about rhyming, verses, or anything else you associate with "songs." It's your song, to be sung in this moment, about how you're feeling now. Once your little song is established, you can let it grow. You can sing any words you want, in any voice you want. Or you might let go of words altogether and just make sounds. Express your feelings through your voice by following your impulses; discover what your voice has to say and sing.

When you feel done, take a moment to process this experience by writing down a few of the highlights: things you found yourself saying that surprised you, different ways you found yourself using your voice, sensations you were aware of in your body. Notice how you feel now compared to how you felt when you started. Are you feeling any relief from your original mood? Have you had any insights?

Great work! For some people this can be a challenging exercise, but I find that it's well worth the effort and the courage. We are all full of history, experience and emotion, and when we give voice to ourselves in this way, we become more complete. We feel new things, we learn new things, and we surprise ourselves.

And when we connect to our emotions, passions and love with our voice we develop a great tool to help us get through our fear of singing. Because Love > Fear! And really, why bother doing this if you're not going to love it?!

Ice Breaker!

Sing the Alphabet

Sing the letters of the alphabet using your own spontaneous melody
or the tune of any song you know, except for the Alphabet Song
you grew up with. Exaggerate the movements of your mouth as you sing
each letter. Try doing it in front of the mirror and watch all the different
movements your mouth and face make as you sing each letter.

Sing it very, very fast and very, very slow, and notice the differences.

Benefits

Allows you to play
in a new way with
familiar sounds.
Exercises and
stretches your
vocal chords and
mouth. Gives you a
chance to sing a wide
variety
of sounds.

Chapter 9
More Fear-Busting Techniques:
Transcending Negative Self-Talk

In the Self-Reflection section of this book in Chapter 4, we explored how negative self-talk pops up when we experience fear. Because this negative self-talk seems to be wired right into our physiology, and has evolved as a means of self-protection, apparently its purpose is to keep us in line in relation to what society expects of us. We are a tribal species. When individuals don't fit into the social norms of the tribe, it can be really bad for the group as a whole.

I think of negative self-talk as the flip-side of free will. It's like a conscience on steroids. The idea of negative self-talk coming from our personal "Gremlins" is useful imagery; it often does feel as if the messages are coming from someone else who lives inside us and "knows better." Thinking in these terms gives us something relatively tangible to work with. Since hearing these negative voices is automatic for most of us, the key is in how we handle them. If we were to take these negative ideas very seriously, we might never try anything new or challenging.

We humans have developed innumerable methods for dealing with our negative self-talk; they can be found in religions around the world as part of the practice of prayer. Self-talk, both negative and positive, has the power to affect our spiritual enlightenment. People use positive self-talk to become better public speakers, to heal themselves from illness, and to relieve stress. Athletes use it in mind-body endurance training. Learning to work in a positive way with negative self-talk makes a powerful difference in the quality of our lives and in how successful we are at our endeavors.

So, when you have been told that you can't sing, and perhaps felt some shame about it, and then you decide that you want to buck the status quo and learn to sing anyway, it's very likely that you're going to be in for a lot of negative self-talk. What can you do about it? How can you deal with it? Luckily, there's a lot that you can do. Here are some suggestions.

"It is more than a curiosity to wonder why there is such a powerful attachment to the negative in the human psyche. One criticism seems to have the power of a dozen compliments. This curiosity is heightened when one considers that many individuals who are plagued by negative self-talk are competent, creative and accomplished."
– Dr. Larry Brooks,
Transforming Negative Self Talk

 . . . .

Remember That You're Not Alone

Everyone in the world has felt unworthy at times. If you can't think of one other person anywhere in the world that you know who has experienced self-doubt and negative self-talk, then you can use me as an example. I testify: I experience negative self-talk on a regular basis, and continuously use an ever-evolving combination of these techniques to get through it. I'm serious.

Let It Out

All this negative stuff can make you sad! We can be so mean to ourselves sometimes and it's a bummer. Go ahead and cry about it if you want. You might feel better.

Photo by Benoît Ferradini / Radio-Canada.

Give Yourself a Break

Think of your nervous, insecure self as a child you are caring for. Visualize rocking your sad, fearful self in your arms as you would a baby. You would never think of telling this sweet baby that he or she wasn't good enough, would you? Do the same for yourself. Give yourself some real compassion.

Use Positive Talk to Create Your Own Luck

Negative self-talk usually goes something like this: "I'm such an idiot," "I'm ugly," "I sound terrible," "I'll never find a girlfriend," "I can't believe I said that," "I'll never get that job," etc. The negative message about the job, for example, could convince you not to apply for it, or to not give it your best shot, because it's encouraging you to sabotage your own efforts. It is generated by a part of you that is scared.

So what does positive self-talk sound like? Let's look at what you might use to replace those negative messages. The idea isn't to say empty words to yourself, but to gradually replace the undercurrent of negative messages with positive ones, so that over time your subconscious develops a more positive outlook, which opens up all kinds of possibilities. Using positive affirmations in the scenario of applying for a job supports your behavior and choices in a positive way. You're more likely to apply for it; you're more likely to have your act together and present your strongest self. This is how self-fulfilling prophesies work: We create our own luck. Research has shown this to be very effective.

Action Steps for Positive Self-Talk
Step 1: Spend a day or two actively listening to all the negative, unkind messages you are sending yourself and write them down. You can do this in a very general way or concentrate on the negative self-talk that comes up around a specific topic. When you keep track of it carefully, you might be surprised by its intensity and frequency.

Step 2: Use these beliefs as a starting point from which to create your affirmations. Below is an example of negative self-talk transformed into affirmations.

- I'll never get that job: **I have an excellent shot at getting that job!**

- They'll find someone better for the job: **I am well-qualified for this job!** (This might also inspire you to be sure that you've done a great job showcasing your qualifications. Your affirmation nudges you to be better prepared.)

- I'm not good enough: **I know I am a great person for this job.**

- I'm too young (or too old): **I'm the perfect age to do what matters to me.**

- I'm not worthy: **I am valuable.** (When you are aware of your own value, you are more likely to share information about yourself that will make your prospective employer see you as valuable.)

- Things are going to turn out badly: **Things will turn out just fine.**

- If I don't get this job I am screwed: **Even if I don't get this job I will be okay.** (This affirmation allows you to feel less desperate, and because you feel less desperate you appear less desperate, and in your interview you'll be more relaxed, and a more attractive candidate.)

Next, move to thoughts that are completely positive: Whatever happens, I will be okay. Whatever happens, I am worthy. I can see myself getting that job, and it feels great. I am so brave to go out for this great job! I am awesome, and I am going to blow them away.

Now let's think about what positive self-talk around singing might look like:
- My voice is beautiful.
- I am learning to sing on key.
- I have the right to learn and explore.
- I am patient and am learning new skills.
- I have many ways of taking in new information.
- I am courageous and it's so cool that I'm trying something new!
- I am brave and strong to be breaking down old barriers.
- I deserve to sing.
- This is going to be fun!
- Singing is my birthright and I'm gonna claim it!

It may seem silly at first, but over time affirmations have a way of working magic. *Saying them out loud* or *writing them down* is even more magical than just *thinking them.* Do all three!

Talk With a Friend

Usually when we share our stories with friends, they share their own stories right back, and that feels good. Sometimes talking with friends about an assumption we have about ourselves — finding a sympathetic ear for the negative voices of our Gremlins — can bring a real shift in perspective. This is significant, because all that negative self-talk cements our sense of how things are and what we can and can't do; a friend can help you sort out what's real from what isn't. Be thoughtful about who you choose to talk to at first, and be aware that you may have to try this with more than one person. If the first friend you talk to isn't the right friend because he or she isn't able to be positive about your singing aspirations, find someone else; don't be deterred!

Visualize It

This is a little like positive self-talk, only less verbal and more visceral. This is using your imagination to put yourself into the exact place that you want to be in the future. If you want to lead the family in singing the Happy Birthday song to your great-grandfather, picture yourself in the location with everyone around you. There's the cake with the 104 candles on it. People are looking at you with the expressions that you want them to have when they look at you. You start to sing, and the song takes off in exactly the way you wish it would. You enjoy the feeling of people looking at you with surprise, while you're eating the cake, and saying, "Hey, I always thought you couldn't sing! That was great!" The people who know you well are beaming with pride for you, because they know how hard you worked for this accomplishment.

After you've visualized in this detailed, positively charged way, it's really easy to notice when you're tempted by any behaviors that don't fall into line with your goal, or opportunities that you might otherwise have passed up. You've raised your energy and awareness and made your desired outcome much more likely. Do this for 20 minutes, four days in a row. This may sound far-fetched, but I've had such success with this method that I think of it as the goose that lays the golden egg. It's like a special good magic.

Journal It

Another way to deal with negative self-talk is to write it all down. All that nasty stuff you're telling yourself can be poured out of your mind and on to paper. Take this opportunity to bring whatever is in your way into a new light, work out problems, get bad feelings off your chest, ask questions, challenge assumptions, and discharge stress.

This is a tried-and-true method for dealing with negative self-talk. Don't censor yourself. Some people write in a journal every day, because it helps keep them sane and generates so much positive outcome.

Let It Go (or Practice Meditation)

Sometimes it's possible to simply let the negative stuff go. There are times when things just seem to get better on their own. It can happen slowly, so that one day we notice a problem isn't really a problem anymore, or that it's not as intense as it was. Or that it's not getting in our way. What if we could speed up this process? It's a perfectly valid option to simply allow ourselves to be distracted away from negativity and to put our focus elsewhere.

Enter meditation. This is the practice of being in the moment and allowing our thoughts, negative and positive, to drift by like clouds in the sky without getting attached to them. Learning not to cling to our negative thoughts allows for immense freedom. If you're not familiar with meditation, check it out. Many yoga classes include a meditation component. Meditation is the foundation of many religions and philosophies, including Buddhism. It's great and powerful stuff! (Be sure to try the exercises in Chapter 10. They all incorporate meditation techniques. In Appendix IV you'll find some great resources for learning more about meditation.)

Make Friends With Your Gremlins

First, identify some of your personal Gremlins. You might have one that says, "I'm too old," and another that says, "I can't handle new things — they will make me stressed," and yet another that says, "I'm too disorganized."

What if, instead of thinking of these Gremlins as enemies, you were to instead think of them as concerned (though overprotective) friends, that are trying to keep you safe? What might you tell them? I suppose you could say: "Thank you, you're right. I am too old, stressed out and disorganized to take on that challenge. Never mind." And that would be that. I suppose that might be alright — that *could* be what's best for you overall. But another approach is to make friends with the Gremlins and ask them why they say the things they say. Engage them in conversation.

Say you want to try acting in a community theater. Your Gremlin says, "You're crazy! You're too old!" You might ask, "What do you mean? I'm only 50. That's not so old. Why are you saying that to me?" And the Gremlin might say, "Everyone else there is like 20 years younger than you and has acting experience and you don't. And they're better looking than you. And more charming. You're going to forget your lines! I'm worried that you're going to be completely humiliated and feel awful."

"Ohhh ... ," you say. "So you're looking out for me! Well, not everybody on stage will be that experienced or so young, but I suppose you could be right — I might mess up. That could happen." And the Gremlin says, "Yeah, so don't do it. It's a stupid thing to do." Then you say to the Gremlin, "Well, you know what? I think I can handle it. I appreciate your warning, but now that I've thought about it, I think that my desire to do this is bigger than my fear of being embarrassed. So if I bomb I may feel bad but I think I'll get over it pretty quickly. I think I'll be alright. But thanks for sharing your concerns with me." When you develop a friendship with your Gremlin, and see those awful words as coming from a place of caring, they sound very different, and you can work with them.

Dealing with Gremlins seems to be an inevitable part of the human experience, but you can use these tools to change your relationship to them. You can make them less powerful so that they don't interfere with your doing what you want to do.

You might be skeptical, but I'm telling you: this stuff works! It works when you need help with any kind of self-doubt, and it definitely helps with a fear of singing.

Fear-Busting Recap:

Ways to deal with Fear of Singing from Chapter 8
• Feel the love
• Don't let fear stop you
• Stay in touch with the sensations that singing creates in your body
• Remember that singing is about emotion, and that fear is just an emotion
• Allow your fear, and other emotions, to be expressed through your voice
• Work on transforming your shame into mere embarrassment

Ways to deal with Fear of Singing from Chapter 9
• Remember that you're not alone
• Let it out
• Give yourself a break
• Use positive talk to create your own luck
• Talk with a friend
• Visualize it
• Journal it
• Let it go (or practice meditation).
• Make friends with your Gremlins

And remember – Love > Fear!

Photo by Rajeev Mehtaa.
Singer Kabul Rishi from New Delhi, India.

Ice Breaker!
Sing On the Move!

When you walk you're creating a steady beat with your feet on the ground.
Think of this rhythm as a drumbeat, and as backup for your own song.

Make something up or sing something you already know;
whatever you sing can bounce off the pattern created by your steps.
You can learn a lot about rhythm by noticing how your song
fits into the constant rhythm of your steps.

While keeping the pace of your walk steady, try slowing your song down
to half-time, so that there are twice as many steps in each phrase.
Try doubling the speed of your song so that there are half as many steps
in each phrase. Try it while looking at your feet or swinging arms to get visual
feedback on how the rhythm of your steps relates to the song you're singing.

Benefits
Helps develop
a sensory
understanding
of rhythm.
When you feel
the rhythm of
a song in your
body, you can
sing it with
more confidence
and conviction.

Chapter 10
The Singing Body Connection

Freedom to Play

There is a place for critical thinking and analysis in this program. There will be times when we will focus on getting it right and singing on pitch. If your goal is to learn to sing with or for other people, you'll want to know how to sing in tune. That will entail practicing specific skills and using some analytic discretion as you compare one sound, one note, with another. Many of the exercises we'll be doing later on will take you into this attitude of study, where you will be measuring your skills and your progress. But it is equally, if not more, important to have times when you are free from the judgements of your critical, analytical mind. That's why the suggestions and exercises in the last two chapters are so important. And now, in this chapter, you'll learn more about how to develop a sense of freedom and joy by working with the connection between singing and the body.

How can you discover your voice and your sound if you don't play with it freely? How can you concentrate on learning the skills of singing when you are too constricted from stress and worries about how you sound to make much of a sound at all? Working through fears and self-consciousness helps bring you into a state of mind where you can explore, play, and learn. We free our voice by learning to relax and enjoy the moment, so that we become familiar with who we truly are vocally. Once you understand how to get into a state of vocal comfort and freedom, you'll be better able to focus on the skills of listening and to use your voice in a connected, purposeful way. Rather than cringing when something comes out differently than you intended, you'll be able to process feedback in a constructive way. And instead of feeling horrified because you've done something wrong, you'll be interested, engaged and curious about your own learning process. And you'll be having fun! Honest!

As I've said, singing, like language, usually comes easily to young children when they are immersed in musical environments and given the freedom to play and explore. Singing will come more easily to *you* if you shed your grown-up persona and preconceptions, and approach your practice with the curiosity and playfulness of a child.

"With every year of playing, you want to relax one more muscle. Why? Because the more tense you are, the less you can hear."
– Yo-Yo Ma

Tip

As you go through this program I'm going to ask you to do some pretty silly things. You won't get the most out of these activities if you take yourself too seriously!

Beginner's Mind

Picture a tiny baby looking around at the leaves on the trees around him. He is feeling the air on his skin, hearing the rustling of the leaves in the breeze, the birdsong, people talking, footsteps, the beating heart of the parent holding him. He has not been told what's important to pay attention to and what's not. Everything is new and fresh. He sees, hears and feels it all without judgment.

Imagine a three-year-old playing in a creek. See how she's touching the water as it moves, splashing in the pools, feeling the rocks with her toes? She's curious to see how the water reacts to her touch, how it feels as it slides through her fingers, how it feels colder in some places and warmer in others, how it splashes when she stomps her feet.

Can you remember back to times in your childhood when you felt unselfconscious, free and full of awe? As children we lived in a world where we experienced each moment fully and openly — we saw everything with fresh eyes. We can still do this.

There is a Buddhist concept called Beginner's Mind. This is a practice of seeing the world as though you've never seen it before, as if everything is new. And in reality, each moment truly is unlike any other. We are, at every moment, offered the opportunity to experience enthusiasm, beauty, creativity and awe. You don't have to pretend in order to be in Beginner's Mind; you just need to let go and experience what *is*, in this very moment.

Beginner's Mind is a great place to be. You are there when you're involved and loving what you're doing so much that it feels like play. You're there when you're awed with the beauty of the world around you, when you're amused by little surprises, when you're noticing how nice the warm water feels on your hands even though you thought you hated doing dishes.

When you let go of preconceptions, of ideas of what singing is or should be, it allows you to be in Beginner's Mind as you discover the unique beauty of your own voice. In this state of mind it is easier to let go of voices that tell you that you can't sing or that you sound bad. Enjoy yourself and let go of thinking in terms of right and wrong.

The following exercise is a very cool way to discover the orientation of Beginner's Mind, and will help you move back into the mindset of the exploring child.

Jon Kabat-Zinn, the founder of the Stress Reduction Clinic at the University of Massachusetts Medical School in Worcester, developed this great exercise to introduce his clients to mindfulness meditation to help them cope with stress. I believe this is a perfect exercise for someone who is anxious about singing. Getting through your fear of singing happens through sinking fully into the moment, into your body, into joy, and by getting away from preconceived ideas about what you should sound like and even about what singing *is*. I know I'm repeating myself, but this is so fundamental and important that it bears repeating. And repeating.

Exercise 10.1: Beginner's Mind Raisin Meditation
(Listen to Track 8 for an audio version of this exercise) 🔊

Preparation: You'll need a comfortable quiet place to stand or sit, and a raisin.
Note: If you don't like raisins, you can use another fruit.

Make yourself comfortable. Pick up the raisin and hold it in your fingers ...

1. Look at it as if you've never seen one before: notice everything you can about this raisin. Notice its shape, texture, size, color.

2. Touch it: Notice how it feels in your fingers. Does it feel hard or soft; squishy or resilient?

3. Smell it: Words may come to mind (e.g., earthy, pungent); acknowledge them, and then go back to the actual sensation of smell.

4. Notice your own reaction to the raisin. Are you having an urge to eat it? Is your mouth watering? Is it difficult to resist an urge to just eat it already?!

5. Put it in your mouth and let your tongue explore the raisin.

6. Bite down once and pause: Notice the taste. Notice how the taste makes your mouth feel.

7. Chew the raisin slowly: notice the taste and the texture. Feel how it's soft yet resistant. Feel the soft membrane of skin over its soft insides. Notice how the sensations change as you chew.

8. Swallow the raisin.

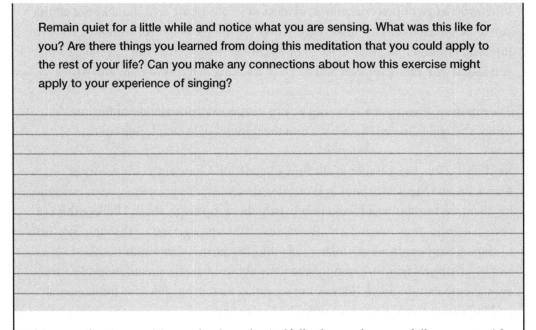

Remain quiet for a little while and notice what you are sensing. What was this like for you? Are there things you learned from doing this meditation that you could apply to the rest of your life? Can you make any connections about how this exercise might apply to your experience of singing?

This way of eating a raisin, so slowly and mindfully that we become fully present with all the sensations we're experiencing, brings to light the extent to which we miss out on things by not paying attention. Things that have become old hat don't have to be that way; nothing has to be boring or ordinary. We can choose to dive in and experience the wonder of what is all around us at any time.

We can use this Beginner's Mind awareness to more deeply experience our voices too. Like the raisin in the exercise you just did, your voice has nuances and textures that you have to slow down to notice. We talk all day long, but usually don't pay much attention to our own voice. We don't notice it vibrating in our chest, throat, face and mouth. We don't pay attention to the quality of its sound. We don't notice how our voice connects to our breath, how it starts deep inside of us and moves up through us and out into the world. By using the Beginner's Mind approach you can tune in to all this richness. You can experience your voice the way the little girl playing in the creek experiences being in the water.

As you proceed through this program, try to keep in touch with the fully present, non-judgemental spirit of the Beginner's Mind. It will make the exercises more productive and more fun.

Breathing, Stretching and Relaxing

When you sing, your body is your musical instrument. Singing works best when your muscles are relaxed, you are breathing deeply and comfortably, and you are feeling connected to your whole body.

I always start my classes and workshops with some yoga-style stretches and breathing, because this helps us relax and increases our lung capacity. It helps bring us into the "zone," that place where we are more in the moment and less self-conscious. As we breathe and stretch together, we tune in to how we are doing right at this moment on a very basic level. We bring ourselves into a place of Beginner's Mind in relation to ourselves (rather than in relation to a raisin). What is our state of mind in this moment? How do our bodies feel? Where we are holding tension? (Often our reaction is, "Wow! I had no idea I was holding so much tension!") What stresses that might have collected during our day can we let go of so that we can pay attention to what we are doing now? We breathe, we relax, we become more centered and solidly present in our bodies and in the moment.

The following are some breathing and stretching exercises that will help you get ready to sing, both physically and emotionally. To start with, try spending at least three to five minutes on each one (or more if you want to) so that you can learn how to do them. These are nice exercises to have on hand for your warm-ups later.

Exercise 10.2: Yoga Stretch with Breath and Sound
Video 3 ▶

Start by standing up, feet solidly planted on the ground. If this is not possible for you, sit comfortably on a chair and scoot a bit towards the front edge so that you can feel your sitz bones against the seat of the chair.

Imagine that while you are standing or sitting, solidly grounded, a string is pulling you up gently towards the sky from the back of the top of your head. Because the string is towards the back part of the top of your head, your chin might be tipped down a little and the front of your neck is even looser than usual. Allow a nice stretch to happen as you are simultaneously pulled towards the earth through your feet or your sitz bones, and towards the sky by the top of your head.

Let your breath deepen and, as you inhale, imagine that you're taking the breath right down into your belly. As you exhale, listen to the sound that naturally happens in your chest and throat. If you're standing and you start to feel a little dizzy, find something solid to hold on to! When you inhale, feel your ribs rise gently up, and as you exhale, imagine that your ribs are staying slightly lifted, creating extra openness under your rib cage, in your lungs, belly, sides and back. Enjoy a sense of spaciousness as you breathe.

After a few breaths like this, begin to bring your arms up along the front of your body as you inhale, imagining that you are sucking in the air the way you would take a delicious drink through a straw. Imagine that your hands are being pulled gently up towards the sky as you finish your inhale. When you are full of breath and ready to exhale, open your arms out widely, arching them over your head and bringing them down to your sides. Make your exhale big enough so that you can hear it.

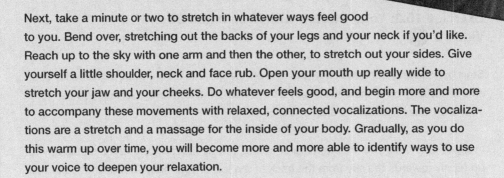

Do this a few times and now begin to vocalize a little on each exhale. You might start with just a hum, or you might make a very low or airy sound, or it might be like a yawn. It might be like a hum with your mouth open. Do it in whatever way feels most comfortable to you. Your vocalization might be an "aaaahhhh" sound, or an "ohhhhh" or an "eeeeeehh." Any sound you make is perfect as long as you are feeling relaxed, natural and comfortable. Do this for a minute or two, or longer if you feel like it. Stop when you feel done.

Next, take a minute or two to stretch in whatever ways feel good to you. Bend over, stretching out the backs of your legs and your neck if you'd like. Reach up to the sky with one arm and then the other, to stretch out your sides. Give yourself a little shoulder, neck and face rub. Open your mouth up really wide to stretch your jaw and your cheeks. Do whatever feels good, and begin more and more to accompany these movements with relaxed, connected vocalizations. The vocalizations are a stretch and a massage for the inside of your body. Gradually, as you do this warm up over time, you will become more and more able to identify ways to use your voice to deepen your relaxation.

This will bring you into a relaxed state of mind, and will begin to integrate your body and your voice. By bringing your voice into the stretches, you're starting to get to know it while using it in a very relaxed way. You're also beginning to see how using your voice can be soothing, and can help your whole body to relax. The goal is to have this feel good, so if there is part of this that is not feeling good to you, let it go and work with what does feel good.

The next exercise is similar to the last, but now you will allow your voice to play a leading role. Both of these exercises are an opportunity to explore your voice, warm up your vocal chords and all the muscles that are involved as you sing, and build your consciousness around using your voice in a bigger way.

Exercise 10.3: Sirening & Movement
Tracks 9 (with instruction) & 10 (no instruction) 🔊 Video 4 ▶

As in the previous exercise, plant your feet solidly on the floor, or your bottom solidly on your chair. Inhale, once again bringing your arms up in front of you so that when you are full of breath, your arms are above your head, reaching up towards the sky. As you begin to exhale and bring your arms back down, make the sound "aahhh" starting at a high pitch when your hands are up and lowering your pitch as you lower your arms down towards your sides. You are in essence making a big loud happy sigh, which involves not only your voice but also your body. Do this a few times. Enjoy the feeling of sliding your voice from high to low.

Now imagine you're a child pretending to be a fire-engine. You're going to make a siren sound using whatever vowel sound (aaah, ooooh, eeee, etc.) best captures for you the essence of "fire-engine." Move your hands, arms and body to illustrate. Give this sound some power and volume and play with what it feels like to go from high to low and then back up again. Continue to comfortably illustrate your sound with your movements as you siren your voice up and down, up and down.

Next, use your voice while imagining a child on a swing, moving back and forth and up and down, increasing a little bit with each repetition. Move your hands in the air to illustrate the movement of the swing.

Now, work with whatever images come to your mind that suggest movement, and follow them with your voice — waves on the ocean, birds soaring in the sky, or riding a roller coaster.

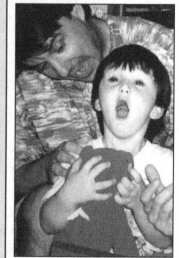

My son Jacob and husband Forrest, circa 2002, having a fire engine moment.

Notice the sensations in your body as your voice moves up and down. Notice how your throat feels, notice how the air feels around your arms and your head. How does making these sliding, siren sounds feel in your face? Approach this like a meditation, with your consciousness as much in the present as possible. Let go of any worry about whether you're getting it right or wrong. This is not about right or wrong. This is about feeling it. Notice and be curious.

You might find that your voice cracks a little bit as you siren. This is very common and nothing to worry about. Try sirening more gently. Try doing it with more energy and power. Notice what happens. Notice without judgement. Play with it.

If you want some companionship while you're doing this, use Track 10, which has lots of sirening and no talking, and do it with me. Or watch Video #4. You can mirror what I'm doing or you can use what I'm doing as a bouncing-off place. Have fun with it.

If any thoughts or feelings have arisen during the last two exercises, you can write about them here.

_____

_____

_____

_____

_____

_____

_____

_____

_____

_____

_____

_____

_____

_____

_____

Exercise 10.4: Floppy Twist
Video 5 ▶

Stand and feel your weight extend solidly into the ground through your feet. (Or, if you are sitting, get yourself solidly planted on your sitz bones. This will work better on a stool, or a chair without arms.) As in the previous exercises, feel the lift from the back of your head up to the sky. Allow your rib cage to lift and expand as you inhale, and allow the spaciousness you've created around your lungs and belly to remain as you exhale. Let your breath be relaxed and natural.

Allow your knees to bend a little and begin to twist gently from side to side. Gradually let your twist grow in size, keeping your arms loose and floppy, like empty coat sleeves. Include your head in the twist, and with each twist, let your head turn around with the rest of your torso and shoulders so that your gaze moves to face the side or the back. Pattern your breathing so that you're inhaling as you face front and exhaling each time you twist around to the back; let your arms swing through the air as you twist and let your hands flop against your body. Your breaths will be light and short, energetic but relaxed, with a little puff on the exhale.

Begin to illustrate your twists with a little sound. You might say "whap" as your hands flop against your body, or "pahh" or "uhhh." Whatever feels right to you is exactly the right thing to do. Do this for a minute or so, until it feels right to stop. Take a break if you feel dizzy — I don't want you to fall down!

This is a good way to loosen up the muscles in your waist and rib cage, and to relax your arms, shoulders and neck. It also creates an energized and powerful breath, and engages your voice in a way that's very connected to your movement.

Exercise 10.5: Side Stretch with Voice
Video 6 ▶

Start with the same standing (or sitting) posture as you used in the previous exercises. Now reach up with your right arm, as though a string was pulling you up through your middle finger as you reach for the sky. Feel a nice stretch all along your right side, in your hip, waist, ribs, neck, arm and hand. Move around a little bit as you adjust the stretch in ways that feel good. Breathe in and out deeply as you stretch, and as you exhale, make any sounds that feel natural. Moans, groans and sighs are great. Most of us are at least a little bit stiff, and this stretch usually targets at least a few tension-holding spots. The job of your voice right now is to massage, from the inside, any spots that need a little extra help releasing. Do this again, raising your left hand toward the sky. Repeat as desired.

Next is an exercise much like the Raisin Meditation, but instead of a raisin, you'll be exploring your voice with a Beginner's Mind.

Exercise 10.6: Beginner's Mind — Beginner's Voice

Lie on the floor and take a few breaths through your nose. Imagine that you are about to break the silence with the very first hum you've ever made or heard. Like the three-year-old exploring water in the stream, like the raisin eater, you have never done this before. You're relaxed and curious. After about three or four breaths, begin to hum as you exhale, quietly, with your mouth closed. What parts of your body do you feel moving? Where in your body do you feel the hum? Is the feeling of humming bringing up any emotions? Does it bring with it any associations, memories or images? Keep breathing and humming. Try moving the hum up and down in pitch and notice if it feels any different, or if you're feeling it in different parts of your body as your pitch changes. Try humming louder and then more quietly again and notice any changes. If you have any urge to rock or move your body, go with it.

Hummmmm ... So how was all this? Write any comments about these activities and how they worked for you below.

This is great! You're starting to make some sound. You're using your voice and muscles together in new ways, expanding your lungs and stretching and strengthening your vocal chords. You're exploring new territory. I hope this felt wonderful! This stretching, deep breathing and vocalizing, especially when done with a Beginner's Mind perspective, can relax you and begin to bring you into the zone, that place where you are in the present, connected to your body and more able to let go of self-criticism. So much of singing has to do with being in a relaxed and open state of mind, and warming up your whole body along with your voice is key.

Tip

These exercises make great warm-ups for whenever you're getting ready to sing. Learn more about warming up in Chapter 20 and Appendix I.

They don't have to be a big deal. Even if you're in the car, or somewhere else where you can't do an official warm-up, you can adapt your favorite exercises from this chapter to whatever setting you're in. Let this orientation of moving slowly, and of noticing and accepting what is happening in your body, be your starting place whenever you're getting ready to sing.

Chapter 11
Listening for Singing

Listening Fully

For those who haven't done much singing, it might not be apparent just how integral the act of listening is to singing, and especially to singing with other people. That's part of the beauty of it and part of what makes singing feel so good. You're taking in and giving out at the same time; it's a conversation.

You may think that you already know how to listen, but you may not know how to listen for singing. It takes a special kind of listening to recognize the notes in a song you are trying to learn. When you find yourself in the moment, trying to learn or sing your song, perhaps surrounded by other voices or instrumental accompaniment, you may feel confused. Making the connection between what you hear and what you are singing can be overwhelming at first, but with practice, you will understand and feel the relationships.

To improve and widen your listening skills, let's start in the non-analytical state of Beginner's Mind, which we began to explore in the Raisin Meditation on page 103. I want you to experience listening in the broadest possible way, in your most accepting state. Soon we will get to the work of analyzing which notes are higher and lower so that you can match a pitch, and listening to how notes transition from one into another so that you can navigate your way around a song. But for now, we'll simply get centered in the world of listening to sound by honing the skill of noticing it in a very present way.

Listening With Beginner's Mind

Before you could understand words you were hearing, you heard them as pure sound. You picked up on the highs and lows in terms of pitch, the loud and soft in terms of volume and the vibe in terms of emotional content. You not only heard sounds, but you felt them as vibrations. During your first days on this earth, you could hear a door opening or closing without associating it with someone coming or going. You could hear an engine starting without associating it with the idea of a car. When you heard a lullaby sung to you or the cooing of a loving parent, you recognized the good feeling without knowing cognitively what was going on.

"As a child, you respond physically, tactically. You're delighted by sound, you're delighted by recognizing something. It's like hide and seek. Is it there? Is it not there? Is it this note? Is it not this note? It's one fantastic game."
– Yo-Yo Ma

Exercise 11.1: Listening with a Beginner's Mind

In this exercise, imagine that you are in this state of infancy now. As much as possible, forget what you know and leave your thinking mind behind. Return to a place of listening and feeling without interpreting. Don't expect yourself to be able to completely empty your mind of thoughts — that would be impossible; just do it as much as you can.

Find a comfortable place to sit or lie down. Close your eyes, notice your own breathing and settle in as comfortably as you can. Begin to notice all of the sounds around you. No sound is more important than another. You may hear a car driving along the street outside, people talking in another room, the hum of a refrigerator, the sound of your own breathing or your cat rubbing against a bedpost. You might hear your clothes moving against your skin as you breathe in and out. Even when you can't identify any outside sound, there's the sound that your ears pick up from the vibrations in the air. Notice and savor each of these as you would savor a taste, or a beautiful view. These are the sounds of your world.

Do this for five to 10 minutes, or longer if you want to. When you are satisfied, jot down as many of the sounds as you can remember, or your overall impressions from this experience, noticing the sound of your pen against the paper, or the keys of your keyboard as you type. Check out W. A. Mathieu's wonderful *The Listening Book: Discovering Your Own Music*, for more exercises like this.

I did this exercise at the hair salon recently and it was absolutely astounding. As I lay back with my head on the edge of that comfortable rounded hairdresser sink I closed my eyes. I tuned my attention into the sounds all around me, not prioritizing any sounds over any others, not interpreting what I was hearing or following the threads of any separate conversations, but rather letting all the sounds blend into one sound experience. It turns out that the hair salon is a perfect place to do this exercise! I enjoyed it the way someone might enjoy hearing a symphony.

I was relaxed and comfortable; my eyes were closed. The sounds of hair dryers, footsteps, chairs being moved, water running, the clinking and clacking of tools and glasses; the constant hum of voices in conversation from which would emerge the most amazing sentence fragments (sometimes very funny!) all wafting in and out of my hearing and consciousness. What a delicious collage of sound and imagery. Listening in this way is a wonderful form of meditation and very relaxing!

Exercise 11.2: Active Listening with Music

This exercise has a lot in common with the last one, but with a very different result. This time you will be listening and then analyzing what you are hearing. Choose a piece of music that you like. It can be any kind of music — a classical piece, a rock and roll song, hip-hop, rap, jazz or avant-garde — anything that you enjoy and find interesting.

Start the same way you did in the last exercise, listening to all the sounds in the music, again without judging, categorizing, or prioritizing. Listen to the whole song that way, once through.

Now play the song again, but this time let your mind notice and follow the threads. Bring what you hear into your consciousness by asking yourself questions. Choose just one question to answer at a time. Don't clutter your mind by listening for too many things at once. Some possible questions could be:

• What different instruments am I hearing?

• What are the highest sounds I hear, or the lowest?

• What rhythmic patterns do I hear?

• Is there singing? If so, is it one voice alone or several together?

You may notice several tunes being played or sung at the same time, or hear more than one note at a time. If you do, get curious about how these tunes and notes are relating to each other. Play the song again and listen just for that. Listen to the song in this way a few times.

Next, listen to the song again and take notes. Jot down the questions you asked and the answers you've discovered.

Tip

By practicing these exercises you are developing the skill of active listening, which is an important step in learning to sing. The more you practice, the easier and more natural it will become for you to listen to music in this way. This ability will be of immense help as you begin to introduce your own voice into the mix! When you are singing with other people, it will be easier to hear them clearly, and find your own place.

Listening and Singing

Next, let's tune into your intuition and free up your sense of vocal play. This can be tough for those convinced that they can't sing; it can even be difficult for experienced singers to do this! Our primary orientation here is that there is no such thing as a mistake. Every single thing you do is right — perfect, in fact — and is the only thing to be done in this moment. Let this be your guiding principle as you move into this exercise. It is designed to draw out your unique expression in response to what you are listening to. Trust your intuition as you explore.

In this exercise we are activating your hands, arms, and voice to respond to the music as you listen. We're tapping into your sense of the profound — your unique soul-music!

Exercise 11.3: Listening and Responding Expressively

Put on a piece of music that moves you. Any genre is fine. Turn the music on and lie down in a comfortable place. As you listen to the music let your arms rise into the air and let your fingers, hands and arms do a dance for you. Illustrate the music with your movements; make your motions larger as the music is larger and smaller as the music is smaller. Be dramatic! Feel all the emotions that the music stirs in you and let them be expressed in your arms. When your feelings and impulses start to outgrow your arms' capacity for expression, start allowing your voice to join in, as quietly or loudly as feels right.

Continue to follow your impulses and make space for your voice to play a bigger and bigger role.

You may want to sing boldly along to the music, or you might be more comfortable just humming along under the surface of what you're hearing. You might hear or sense a direct connection between your vocal expression and the music you're listening to, or they may feel separate. You may notice moments of harmony, when what you're singing sounds nice to you, but you might not. Whatever you're doing, it's absolutely fine. You're dipping your foot into the world of improvisation. You're exploring the language of music in exactly the way that a baby starts to explore his native language; you're listening, trying it out yourself, feeling how you fit in, and then doing it some more.

Do this for just a little while, or keep going. Put on another song if you want to. Sing along, get quiet, get loud, get up and move around or get up and dance if you want to, keeping your voice involved in whatever ways feel best. Feel the groove and be part of it. That's it. It's a simple thing to do. The tricky bit is doing it without allowing any judging voices to get in the way of your hearing, your exploration or your joy.

You are making connections between the feelings that listening produces in you (both physically and emotionally) and how your reactions are being manifested in your outward expression. Remember that there is no right or wrong here. If you have chosen a rock and roll song for this exercise, what comes out of you may look and sound very different than if you'd chosen a piece by Vivaldi. Your song and dance could never look just like someone else's song and dance. This expressive improvisation is completely unique to you.

You may never before have brought your voice into the realm of personal expression like this. Later on, when you are singing songs, I hope you will tap into this capacity to deeply and spontaneously express yourself using your voice.

How did it go? Write about it here.

_____

_____

_____

_____

_____

_____

_____

"Even the most inexperienced player can be a wonderful improviser, because the sources of great improvisation are heart and soul."
— James Oshinsky
Return to Child, The Music for People Improvisation Guide

Now, on to the science of sound in our bodies!

Ice Breaker!

Listen, and Copy with Your Voice

Try this with any and all kinds of sounds. Car sounds, animal sounds,
squeaky doors, alarm clocks, ring tones or opera singers.
See how closely you can mimic both the sound and *feeling* of the sound.

Benefits

Hones listening and
imitation skills, both
very beneficial for
singing!

Chapter 12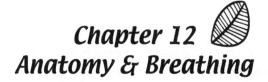
Anatomy & Breathing

Your Vocal Apparatus, Breath, Attitude, Posture, and Some Tricks

Singing is a whole-body activity. If that's a new thought for you, take a minute to digest it. Try this: take a deep, relaxed breath. Relax your shoulders. Make your belly big and soft, like a bellows. Think Buddha, not fashion model. Now, for contrast, try holding in your stomach tight and taking a deep breath. Look down as you do this and see what happens to your chest and shoulders — you can see them rise and fall. The breath is trapped up in the top part of your body. Your shoulders tense up. Your throat tightens. This is not a good way to breathe for singing. It tenses muscles that would be better to let relax instead.

Now take a few deep breaths with your stomach muscles all relaxed and loose. Forget every idea you have about how it's good to have a small, flat stomach. As you breathe with a relaxed belly, look down again to see what's moving. Your stomach puffs up big and then gets smaller when you exhale. Your upper chest and shoulders move much less. This is the way to do it. Deep belly breaths. Even your lower back seems to expand with each breath. Relaxed shoulders, relaxed neck, relaxed throat. It's easy and grounded. It feels good.

Your Body is a Wind Instrument

Your posture, the movement of your abdominal and diaphragmatic muscles, and your breath are very helpful things to be aware of when you sing. Your body is a wind instrument, and needs a good flow of air coming in and out to work right. You need good alignment (posture) so that your airways and lungs have plenty of unobstructed space to move and gather air as you breathe in, and you need to engage your stomach and diaphragmatic muscles to push the air back out past your vocal cords to produce sound.

Breath is to using your voice as gas is to driving a car. It's the fuel that makes any vocal sound or song possible. You need a good, strong flow of breath to sing comfortably and confidently. When you

Vocal Health Advice From My ENT Doctor:

We all have limited vocal stamina and can easily over-do, especially if we don't build up slowly. If you find yourself getting hoarse or developing a sore throat, take a break and let your vocal cords rest! Come back when you feel better and maybe this time you can go a little longer, louder or higher.

If you have REFLUX you may be subjecting your vocal cords to constant irritation. If your throat bothers you a lot when you sing, check into that, okay?

Drink a lot of water. Your vocal cords are supposed to be covered with a nice coat of mucus — when you aren't properly hydrated that dries out and it is harder to sing.

Take good care of your voice!

try to sing without enough breath you're likely to feel dizzy, unable to sing on key or to concentrate, and you might even feel slightly panicky. It's as though you're running out of gas; something is wrong. Breathing deeply also helps you relax and get into the zone so that you are able to enjoy yourself more as you sing.

If we're tense or scared, our breathing tends to get short and shallow. When all is well, we're more likely to breathe deeply. If you're nervous about singing, your body's automatic reaction may be to tighten up and shorten the breath, restricting it to your upper chest. We can counteract this tendency by remembering to breathe fully, keeping our stomach and diaphragmatic muscles engaged and moving. In turn, we'll feel more relaxed and fearless. Breathing is completely integral to singing. No breath, no voice. Strong open breath, strong open singing!

You may have heard the expression "breathing from the diaphragm" or "supportive breath." This is a great thing for you to know about, and an extremely useful tool for beginners. After a brief overview of your vocal anatomy, we will get right to some great exercises to show you what all this breath talk is about.

Three Main Parts Are Involved in the Production of Voice

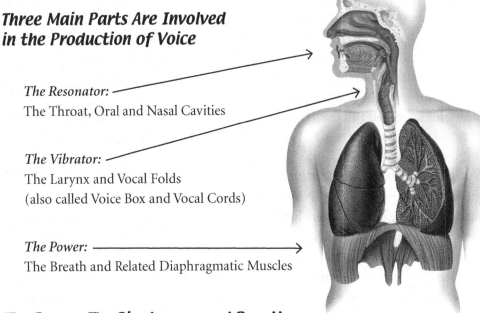

The Resonator:
The Throat, Oral and Nasal Cavities

The Vibrator:
The Larynx and Vocal Folds
(also called Voice Box and Vocal Cords)

The Power:
The Breath and Related Diaphragmatic Muscles

The Power: The Diaphragm and Breath

The diaphragm is a big, dome shaped layer of muscle and tendon, the top of which lies horizontally below your lungs, and the sides of which sit like a wide belt around the inside of the whole bottom half of your rib cage. The diaphragm is shaped kind of like a parachute. Like everything about our body its functionality is complicated, but simply put, the diaphragm and related muscles are main actors in the body's breathing process, and it's helpful to have a general idea of how they work.

The "belt" part of the diaphragm that lies next to the ribs squeezes in and pushes out as you breathe causing the top of the diaphragm to rise and fall. When breathing in, the belt loosens and the diaphragm flattens out and lowers, making room for the lungs above to fill with air. When exhaling, the belt tightens, pushing the top part of the diaphragm up into a dome shape, pushing the air out and creating a vacuum readying the lungs to take their next breath. It is this motion that pushes and pulls the air in and out of your lungs, and past your vocal cords.

The Larynx and Vocal Folds (or Voice Box and Vocal Cords)

At the top of your windpipe is the part of your throat called the larynx (also called the voice box). At the bottom of the larynx are your vocal folds (also called vocal cords). As a beginning singer, the common misconception that there's something you have to actively *make your vocal folds do* can cause unnecessary tension in your throat, neck and shoulders. You'll benefit more from an orientation of observation than one of trying to boss your vocal folds around. Ask, "What do I notice happening in my throat when I sing high versus low, or when my voice is narrow and focused versus airy and loose?" Just noticing is a great practice.

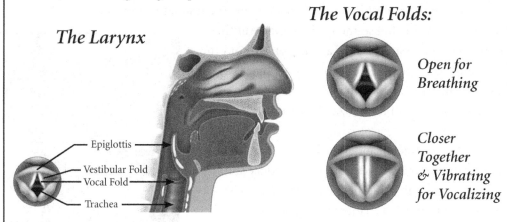

The Larynx

Epiglottis
Vestibular Fold
Vocal Fold
Trachea

The Vocal Folds:

Open for Breathing

Closer Together & Vibrating for Vocalizing

The vocal folds lay horizontally across the bottom of the vertical, tube-shaped larynx. Although the term "vocal cords" is commonly used, it can be misleading because they aren't like the separate cords or strings on a cello; they are two bands of muscle and ligament covered with soft skin, and attached at the sides with a space in between. They are sort of like a set of soft, rubbery doors in the windpipe that open and close, locking air out or letting air through. When you are breathing and not making any vocal sound, your vocal folds are open so that breath can pass through freely. When you swallow, the folds come together tightly so that food doesn't go down the wrong tube. When you use your voice the vocal folds are set into a very fast vibrating motion by the breath passing through the windpipe. The vocal folds adjust their length, thickness and tension, along with the frequency of their vibration as air passes through them, determining the pitch of your voice.

Our whole throat is made up of muscles but only very specific muscles are responsible for moving the vocal folds in a way that determines pitch. Again, the tendency for people to feel as if they need to do more than is actually necessary with their throats can cause lots of unhelpful tension. Having a tight throat won't help you to sing higher or lower, or to sing more in tune. It will only give you a tighter, more closed sound and cause you to tire more quickly. It will also make singing less physically comfortable and enjoyable.

Unfortunately, a fear of singing can easily lead to tension in the throat, due to a conscious or unconscious reflex to hold back for a variety of emotional reasons, or due to a mistaken idea that you will be more in control of what comes out if you hold yourself tightly. The tendency to tense up the throat is totally understandable, but unhelpful nonetheless. It's extremely beneficial to relax and that's good news — less is more!

The Resonators: The Throat, Mouth and Nose

Alone, the vibration of the vocal cords produces only a small, buzzing sound. Imagine a taut string being plucked in mid-air, versus a guitar string laid along the body of a guitar. It's the vibration of the wooden box, the resonator, and the air inside it that makes the big full sound of the guitar. Another example is the mouthpiece of a trumpet; without the rest of the trumpet the mouthpiece only makes a small sound. The rest of the trumpet is the resonator, which gives us the full and recognizable trumpet sound.

Our resonator tract includes the chest, throat, mouth, nasal passages and sinuses. When we produce sound this whole system including the air inside those spaces is set to vibrating and changes the buzz of the vocal cords into the full sound that is our voice. It's interesting to think about all the different variables involved; the unique combinations of size, texture and shape of each person's anatomy is what makes each person's voice different from anyone else's. In the same way that we recognise a person's face because it's a unique combination of a multitude of detailed characteristics, we can often recognize who someone is by their voice without seeing them, for the same reason.

Advanced singers often manipulate parts of the vocal tract (placement of the larynx, lifting or lowering the soft pallet, raising their cheekbones, shaping their mouth, etc.) to achieve the voice quality they want. But for the beginning singer the important thing is to start with good postural alignment, to relax enough to discover what feels comfortable, and to explore as a way of learning to get the kind of sound you want.

Working with the Breath

The diaphragmatic muscles and your breath are the power source of singing. Knowing that the diaphragmatic muscles have you covered and are ready and able to do the heavy lifting can help you to take the focus off your throat so you can relax it. Consciously working with the diaphragmatic muscles can be very helpful when singing, giving you more power, control and comfort. Even a quick, light pat on the belly, can be a great prompt for you to shift your focus, reminding you to access the strength of your diaphragm and related muscles, while releasing any tension in your neck, throat, jaw and face.

The following exercise will help you understand in a visceral way what it means to breathe from the diaphragm, and it's very simple.

Exercise 12.1: "SS–SS–SS–SS–SS–SS–SS–SS–SS–SSSSsssssssss …"
(This is a very important exercise that I do with ALL my students!)
Video 7 ▶

Take a nice, big relaxed breath and feel it fill your lungs while you allow your belly to expand. Check in to be sure that your shoulders, neck and jaw are relaxed. While you are still full of air, begin to make an "sssssss" sound, like a child pretending to be a snake. Make repeated short "sss" sounds that repeat until your breath is used up. Begin to notice what parts of your body seem to be engaged and working as you do this.

Repeat, again double-checking that your shoulders, neck and jaw are relaxed. This time place your hand over your the top of your belly. Again, exhale on a series of short "sss" sounds until you are out of air.

What parts of your body do you feel engaging and working as you do this? Can you feel the muscles in your upper belly, under your hand, contract and release each time you start and stop the "sss" sound?

Do this a few more times until you are able to clearly identify what this diaphragmatic breathing feels like. If you are having a hard time feeling these muscles working, try exaggerating the action by squeezing in a little bit on the muscles under your hand while exhaling on the "sss" sound. If you are still unclear, try doing this in front of a mirror to give yourself a visual cue.

Do it again one last time. This time, keep exhaling until you feel like you are completely out of breath. You may want to change from the "sss-sss-sss-sss-sss" to a long "sssssssssssss" as you approach the end of your breath. Notice how you have to squeeze your stomach and diaphragm to keep the "ssssssssssssss" sound going. Your diaphragm is squeezing in tighter and tighter as you use up your breath, isn't it? It's amazing how much longer you can go, how much breath you have on reserve, when you push it out with those belly and diaphragmatic muscles!

At the end of this last exhale, you will feel that you are working hard. This is an opportunity to zero in on these muscles. I want you to feel, very clearly, the way the power at the end of this long breath is coming from the diaphragm and belly, and not from the throat, jaw, etc.

Once you've identified when your diaphragmatic muscles are doing the bulk of the work and what that feels like, it means you are free to go ahead and relax everything else. The stomach and diaphragmatic muscles are big and strong; the muscles in your neck and throat are smaller and more delicate. Your throat, neck, jaw and face shouldn't have to do any hard labor; the more flexible and relaxed they are, the better. The strength, power, stamina, and volume of your voice are all relying on the support that comes from your diaphragmatic breathing.

This is a beautiful exercise because it's so simple, and clearly shows you which muscles you need to engage to sing. And by engage, I don't mean that when you are singing you need to tighten up or work hard the way you did at the end of this exercise. Generally, all you need to do is bring a light consciousness to this area that is doing the work of powering your singing. Just remember that it's there to help you, and let everything else relax. In order to make any sound at all, your diaphragmatic muscles are working anyway to some extent. Often it's enough just to remember that.

Sometimes, when you are faltering for some reason (your voice is shaky, you are running out of breath, or feeling tense in your throat or jaw), it can be of immense help to check in to see whether your diaphragm is engaged, and just slightly increase the squeeze there.

More Space than you Realized

The next exercise is designed to help you realize how much space you have to take in air. It's probably more than you realize!

Exercise 12.2: 360° Breathing — Upside Down (Video 8)

Stand with your feet firmly on the ground, and bend over from the waist. Take whatever measures are needed so that if you get dizzy you won't fall. Stabilize yourself if you want to by bracing your hands on your thighs or holding onto a chair or a door frame. Keep your head up so that your face is parallel to the floor. Breathe in and out normally once or twice to get settled in this inverted position. Next, stand up slowly, shake out and relax.

Now that you know how to get into the right position, you can proceed with the rest of this exercise...

• Bend over the way you did before.

• Firmly suck in your stomach muscles — in exactly the opposite way you do in every other exercise in this book!

• Inhale deeply while your stomach muscles are sucked in.

• While inhaling, notice all the places where your breath is forced to go, and notice all the stretching and accommodating that is happening in your muscles and ribs to make space for your breath. Do this a few times while considering the following questions:

 Do your feel your ribs separating and opening?
 Do you feel as if air is filling up your back? Your sides?
 Do your lungs feel bigger and more three-dimensional?

• Relax your belly and slowly stand back up (be aware of any dizziness and hold on to something if you need to).

• Once you are standing and your belly is again relaxed, take a nice big breath, bringing your awareness to those places that you felt expanding with breath when you were upside down. Did you discover more room for breath than you thought there was? Are your ribs stretching and opening more than you thought they could?

Write down your observations here.

Both the previous and the following exercises are great for helping us discover what it feels like to breathe more deeply and access more of our lung power.

Exercise 12.3: 360° Breathing — Standing/Sitting

Take a nice big breath, just like in the earlier exercises, but this time consciously allow your breath to expand into the places that you discovered in the last exercise. Feel the breath filling your belly, sides, back, and ribs, and now exhale on a comfortable, expansive, vocalized "aaaahhhh." Do a few of these, experimenting with both how the inhale feels when it's big like this, and with how the exhale/vocalization feels when you engage the diaphragmatic muscles and give a little squeeze. Remember to keep your shoulders, throat, neck and face nice and relaxed! That's it — enjoy!!

Tip

It's always good to include deep, relaxed breathing in your warm ups, and ideal to combine it with stretches, humming, or sirening. But even if you're simply singing (as opposed to warming up), knowing how to expand your ribs and lungs to bring in more air is a big help.

"Heys"

I love Heys. Heys are great fun and also an excellent opportunity for practicing diaphragmatic breathing. Heys are something you probably do anyway, now and then, unless you're a very polite person. When you're hollering across the street for your kids to come in for dinner, or when you see a friend down the street and you want to get their attention and you yell, "Hey, Alvin," you're using a Hey voice. It's a yell, but not an angry or strident yell. It's not a scream. It's more of a call.

I learned about Heys in the Balkan singing classes I took in the 1980s with Ethel Raim, artistic director of the Center for Traditional Music and Dance in New York City. She would tap out a rhythm on her lap and indicate around the circle as it was each person's turn to call out a loud "Heeeyyy" or a "Heeeeeeyy-Hey!" Sometimes she would pause and work a little longer with somebody, just to help them get their Heys out because this was all so unfamiliar for us. We weren't used to being so loud!

Photo © Maigi | Dreamstime.com.
In traditional singing from the Balkans (Bulgaria, Croatia, and neighboring countries) the voice is used in a full bold way that Americans and Northern Europeans often think of as "nasal."

Ethel was very encouraging and kind, because making a sound like this, in the context of singing, was scary. It's not uncommon to yell to get someone's attention, but we have an idea that singing is supposed to be pretty, and in our culture this sound isn't considered pretty, though it's a frequent element in traditional Balkan singing. So Ethel would go around the room, getting us to make these crazy loud sounds, and it was more liberating than I can say. Then, when other people joined in and we used this strong voice together, we would create an amazing, powerful group sound that was different than anything I'd ever experienced. That was my introduction to Hey.

I think of Heys as a way to break the sound barrier both physically and psychological-ly. Heys are a way to move from a place of shyness or introversion into being out there in the world. A Hey is the voice of assertion. Once you make the statement of a Hey, the ice is broken. It's also like a great big full-body stretch for the voice, and gets those vocal folds working like crazy. If you do it in a relaxed way, just a big kind-hearted and joyous yell, you won't feel any more strain than if you were calling "Hey" to a friend down the street.

So here's how you do a Hey:

Exercise 12.4: "Hey"
Track 11 🔊 Video 9 ▶

Make sure you've done some gentler warm-ups first — breathing, stretching, toning, sirening, etc. (See chapter 8 for ideas.) Have a glass of water on hand. If doing this makes your throat feel tight or strained, refer to exercise 12.1: Sss-Sss-Sss-Sss, for a reminder about engaging your diaphragmatic muscles for more singing power!

Find a solid position, standing or sitting. Take in a nice full belly breath, and look, or pretend you're looking at a spot far away, across the street, across the rooftops to the next street, across a river, across a canyon or across a field, for example; whatever works for you.

Call out, not worrying about the pitch or anything at all, "Heyyyyy!" (Don't overly em-phasize the H — focus more on the "aaayyyy" part of the sound.) You don't need to scream or strain, you just need to relax and let out your natural voice in a big way. Try "Heyyy Youuuuuu.....!" and let your voice trail away.

Experiment and play with this. Just do it for a little while. You may find that you get a little phlegmy and need to clear your throat. That's fine, but clear it gently, and take a sip or two of your water. At first it may feel like enough to do this just a few times. That's all I usually do when I'm warming up, but even that little bit of Hey sets me up to sing in a different way. What seemed out of reach now seems easily accessible, because I've gone to the extreme and it was fine, and fun. Now, when I go into my regular singing, I have access to more range, more volume, and to that joyous, out-there, Hey! energy.

If you'd like to hear some Balkan singing, visit the website for a link.

Skills for Singing
About Chapters 13 - 23

*In Chapters 13-23 we'll be working on developing the skills you'll need for singing.
Again, you can either work through these chapters in order, or pick and choose which
chapters feel relevant to you. You'll learn some basic music theory and vocabulary,
how to create a warm-up routine, how to sing what you hear (matching pitch/singing in tune),
and work on improving your rhythm in relation to singing. You'll gain tools to help you know
how to approach a song, develop a practice routine, and build a repertoire of songs.
These skills are important and rewarding as you move from being a non-singer to a singer.*

*Here's a quick guide to the lessons
and exercises in Chapters 13-23:*

• Some Vocabulary and a Little Theory

• Matching Pitch & Singing with a
  Drone Note

• Audiation

• Singing Scales and Patterns

• How to Approach a Song

• Get the Rhythm in Your Body

• Get the Rhythm in Your Song

• Create an Inspiring Warm-Up Routine

• Repetition, Muscle Memory, and Practicing

• Building Your Repertoire

• Moving Into the Rest
  of Your Life as a Singer

Before diving in, I suggest you
skim each chapter in this section
to see what seems most useful to
you, and then choose whether to
move through the lessons in order
or move through them intuitively.

The ideas in this section do build
on each other but please remember
to honor your own style of learning. If you find yourself getting
overwhelmed or frustrated by a
topic, feel free to move on, knowing that you can return to it at
any time.

An Important Note On Warm-Ups:
*It's important to read Chapter 20: Creating an Inspiring Warm-Up Routine,
because warming up helps protect your voice and makes singing much more pleasurable.
A lot of the exercises throughout this book can be used as warm-ups.
To make it easier for you I've rounded up many of these, along with some new ones,
and put them all into Appendix I. In Appendix II you'll find a handy, dandy warm-up sheet
that you can cut out of the book to carry around or tack to your wall as a reminder.*

Chapter 13
Unlocking the Mystery of Music:
Some Vocabulary and a Little Theory

In every culture music is invented, played and spoken about according to its own specific conventions and rules. You do not need to understand all (or any) of these rules to sing. However, understanding some of these basic concepts can be helpful because they provide another way to understand what you're doing and can help you grasp and visualize the relationships between the notes you're singing.

Having some music vocabulary will also help you communicate with other people, making it easier to sing and play together. If this chapter feels daunting or uninteresting, please skip it for now. You can always come back to it when you're ready. Some of the vocabulary here will show up in other parts of this book, so if you don't read through this chapter now, remember to return to it as needed to check the meaning of words and phrases as you go along.

Demystifying Music Theory

Music theory is a combination of science, art and convention. To a degree, the way a culture organizes its musical structures is arbitrary. Music theory is a language. Just like all other languages, it is comprised of rules made up by human beings to organize what, in nature, simply *is*.

Sound exists. It has certain natural properties. Nature doesn't have a definition of what a note or a scale is; that's something we humans make up. What we define as notes in a scale are merely certain spots along a continuum, based on various observations of the nature of sound. In the same way that a group of people can decide that any sound is a word with a specific meaning and therefore part of their spoken language, so we as a group have defined that certain combinations of sounds form a scale, and are part of our musical system. The musical ideas that follow are extracted from the basic rules that comprise our system of musical communication in western music.

Following is some musical vocabulary along with some basic music theory concepts to help you get started. If you play another instru-

"My idea is that there is music in the air, music all around us; the world is full of it, and you simply take as much as you require."
– Edward Elgar

 . . . .

"It occurred to me by intuition, and music was the driving force behind that intuition. My discovery was the result of musical perception."
– Albert Einstein (When asked about his theory of relativity.)

ment, you may already be familiar with these concepts — if not, you may find that this clears up a few mysteries.

Vocabulary Words and Terms

The following terms are not in alphabetical order. Instead they are organized to create a narrative that will build from idea to idea, and help you gain an overall understanding of how we talk and think about musical concepts.

Music: Sound that is organized in an intentional or meaningful way.

Pitch (and Note): How high or low a note is. "Her voice kept rising in pitch." A pitch is determined by the rate of vibration of a sound wave. A high sound has a faster, shorter sound wave frequency; a low sound has a slower, longer sound wave frequency.

The word "note" is often used interchangeably with the word, "pitch." "The singer held the *note* too long." "Note" is also used to mean the written notation representing the pitch and duration of a musical sound. "I have the sheet music but it's hard to read some of the *notes* because the paper is old and faded."

Melody: An arrangement of notes that make up a musical composition. The main tune of a song as opposed to other elements such as harmony or rhythm.

Sirening (or Sliding): A vocal slide. Think about how the sound of a fire engine siren slides up and down in pitch in a smooth, continuous way. The official word for a musical slide (whether vocal or on an instrument) is "glissando." I like using the word "siren" with beginners because it invites play — which is the attitude we want to have while we're learning. Refer to Track 10 for some examples. ◀))

Our voice is naturally slidey; when we talk we move it up and down in pitch, giving our words inflection and expression. If we didn't slide around, but rather spoke our words on only one note, we'd be talking in a monotone, as if we were pretending to be robots. When we sing (although there is often some sliding involved) most of the time we are sustaining sound at specific spots along the continuum of the siren. Those spots are the notes that create the song. Sirening is a great way to get warmed up and learn to find, or match, a particular pitch with your voice.

Photo by Adam Jones.
Musicians Rock the Park, Memphis Tennessee.

Singing in Tune (or Singing on Pitch):

Generally, this means that you are singing what is intended; either singing the notes that make up the tune (or melody) of a song accurately, or different notes that sound good when they're sung along with the melody (see the definition for "harmony"). Singing in tune means that you are hitting the intended notes pretty much right on, rather than being higher or lower than the intended pitch.

Pitch Matching: The ability to hear a note and then sing it. If you're learning to sing, matching pitch is one of the first things to work on.

Unison: Playing or singing the exact same note or notes at the same time. Listen to Track 5 🔊 to hear unison singing. This often refers to a whole song, or a phrase of a song, rather than to just one note. You can sing a song or a verse in unison (with everyone singing the same notes as you proceed through the song) as opposed to singing it in harmony (different people singing different notes to create a desired effect). Sometimes people sing parts of a song in harmony and other parts in unison.

Harmony: Harmony is when you deliberately sing or play two or more different notes simultaneously to get a desired effect. The melody is the main tune, and then any other parts that join in to support the melody are called "harmonies." Listen to Track 12 to hear some examples of voices singing in harmony. 🔊

Tip

Clearing Up a Common Misconception

Pitch Matching is not the same as **Perfect Pitch**. Perfect Pitch is the rare ability to, out of thin air, identify a specific note without hearing it first. For example, someone with perfect pitch might be asked to sing a G# note, and without a pitch pipe or a piano or any outside cue at all, they can sing that G#. When they walk over to the piano and play a G#, it will be the same as the note they are singing. Or perhaps they'll hear a note on the piano and, without looking, they can name that note.

Most people don't have perfect pitch. It has nothing to do with how good a musician or singer you are, so don't feel discouraged if you don't! You do not need perfect pitch to sing!

The word harmony usually refers to a combination of notes producing a "pleasing" sound, but be aware that "pleasing" is a subjective term. What defines harmony is a combination of science and cultural norms. In western music certain kinds of note combinations are considered harmonious. The mathematical relationships between the frequencies (rate of vibration) of the notes could be said to "agree," meeting up in ways that create a smoothness of sound. In other cultures different combinations of notes might be considered to be good harmony.

Droning (or Toning): Sustaining one note for a long time, often while someone else plays or sings other notes over it. This is something I always do with beginning singers. Listen to Tracks 2 & 3 for examples of a drone. 🔊

Octave: The interval between one musical pitch and another with half or double its sound wave frequency. The octave relationship is a natural phenomenon, recognized in most of the world's musical systems.

Because notes that are an octave apart are exactly double in frequency from each other, our experience when hearing them is that even though one is lower and one is higher, they have a sameness to them. For example, the note we call middle C has a frequency of 261.62 Hertz, An octave below middle C is another lower C note which has a frequency of 130.81 Hz, which is half of the Middle C's 261.62 Hz. An octave above the middle C is a higher C, with a frequency of 523.25 Hz (twice that of middle C). The C that is an octave above that has twice as high a frequency, 1046.50, and so on. Listen to Track 13 to hear to notes sung and played an octave apart. 🔊

Because the keys of a piano show all the notes in a nice sequential way, we will use illustrations of a piano keyboard to show how all this works.

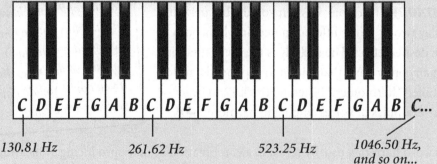

C-Notes an Octave Apart and Their Sound Frequencies

C D E F G A B C D E F G A B C D E F G A B C...

130.81 Hz   261.62 Hz   523.25 Hz   1046.50 Hz, and so on...

Interval: The distance between notes. Intervals can be closer or wider. Examples of closer intervals are the first two notes of "This Land is Your Land," or "Rudolf, the Red Nosed Reindeer." You can find examples of wider intervals in the first two words of "My Bonnie Lies Over the Ocean," or in the syllables "some" and "where" in "Somewhere over the Rainbow." When learning about scales, we will be talking a lot about intervals. Listen to Track 14 to hear some of these examples. 🔊

Familiar Song Intervals

We can listen to the first few notes of familiar songs to hear examples of closer and wider intervals between notes.

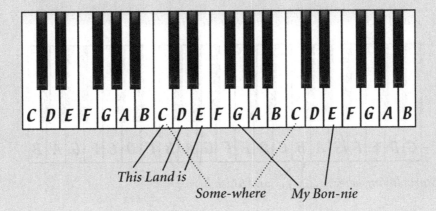

This Land is

Some-where   My Bon-nie

Scale: A graduated series of notes in order from low to high (an ascending scale) or high to low (a descending scale), that comprise the vocabulary from which to play, sing, or create a musical composition. When you hear someone singing, "Do Re Mi Fa So La Ti Do," they are singing a scale in which the first note (Do) is an octave below the last note (the ending Do). The notes in a scale are arranged in a given pattern, with specific, though not always even, intervals between each note.

In any given scale, the same pattern of notes and intervals is repeated from octave to octave. You play it once, from the beginning of the octave to the end (Do to Do), and then you can start over again, proceeding up to the next octave, using the same exact pattern. See chromatic scale, diatonic scale, non-western scales, diatonic major and minor scales and movable scales below. Or don't. Really — if this is freaking you out just come back to it later when you're curious.

Chromatic Scale: If you play every note on the piano in order including all the white and black keys, that's a chromatic scale. Start on any note and then finish on the same note an octave above, and you will be playing the 12 notes of the chromatic scale (plus the final note which is both the end of the octave you're playing and the start of the next octave up).

Play a Chromatic Scale (Track 15) ◀))

To play a chromatic scale on the piano you can start anywhere, just as long as you keep playing the next note up, including both the black and white keys, finishing an octave above where you started.

Play Track 15 and follow along with the illustration.

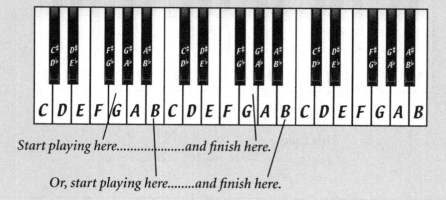

Start playing here...............and finish here.

Or, start playing here........and finish here.

The white keys are called A, B, C, D, E, F, G. The black keys don't get their own letter; they are called the sharps and flats of keys adjacent to them. The illustration above shows the names of all the notes. For more about Sharps and Flats see page 136.

If you have access to a piano or keyboard, play the notes while referring to the illustration above.

The main point here is this: The chromatic scale includes all the notes we have in our Traditional Western music. All the notes in our songs are found somewhere in this scale.

Half Steps and Whole Steps: Each note of the chromatic scale is what we call a "half-step" apart from the next note above or below. The intervals are equal between every half step. If you skip a note, the interval is called a "whole step."

You can easily understand what half and whole steps are when you see them on a piano keyboard. The interval between any two notes that are right next to each other on the piano, whether white or black, is a half-step. When you skip a key, either white or black, the interval is a whole step.

Half-Steps and Whole-Steps

Any two notes that are right next to each other, regardless of whether the keys are black or white, are a half-step apart. Any two notes that have one note between them, are a whole step apart. Count out the examples below to see the different ways that this can look.

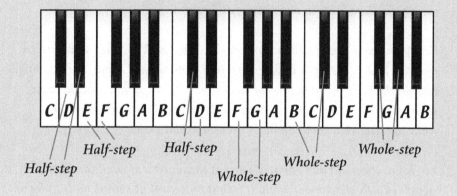

Diatonic Scale: Most Western music is written using what we call the diatonic scale, which consists of a subset of notes taken from the chromatic scale. You are probably already very, very familiar with what a diatonic scale sounds like because almost all the music you hear uses it. For most people familiar with "Western" music, it just feels right.

When you hear someone singing "Do Re Mi Fa So La Ti Do," that classic scale pattern that you might hear the opera singer character practicing in a movie, it's probably the major diatonic scale that they are singing.

The diatonic scale is made up of seven notes. Since there are 12 available notes in the chromatic scale to choose from, we'll have to skip some notes, right? So it's that pattern of notes chosen and notes skipped, and the intervals between them (a specific pattern of half-steps and whole-steps) that defines a diatonic scale. Get it? This is how you get your do-re-mi-fa-so-la-ti-do sound.

There are two main kinds of diatonic scales: major and minor. Right now we're going to talk about the major diatonic scale. (I'll show you something cool about the minor diatonic scale a little later.)

No matter what note you start on, the major diatonic interval pattern is this:

whole-whole-half-whole-whole-whole-half.

Major Diatonic Scales in the Keys of C and A (Track 16)

NOTE: This looks a lot more complicated than it is — it's really all about saying the same thing in a variety of different ways.

Below are examples of two diatonic scales. They both use the same pattern of whole and half-steps, but one starts and ends on the C note (the diatonic scale in the key of C), and one starts and ends on the A note (the diatonic scale in the key of A). The scale that starts on the C uses only white keys while the scale that starts on the A uses some black keys.

But count them out and you will see that the pattern of whole and half-steps is exactly the same in both. It is that pattern that defines both scales as "diatonic." Listen to them on the piano (Track 16) and you'll hear that even though one is higher than the other, they both have the same "tune."

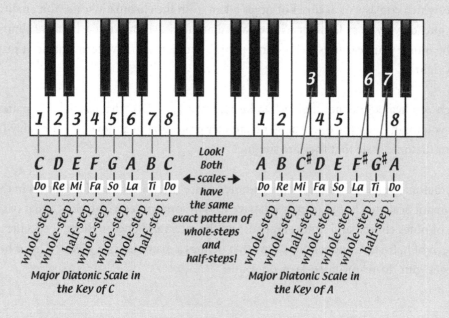

Listen to Track 16 again and follow along with the illustration on the previous page. 🔊))

You will hear me playing and singing the notes of the major diatonic scale in both the key of C and the key of A. I will sing them each in 3 ways:

1. With numbers.

2. With the letter names of each note.

3. With the syllables "Do Re Mi," etc.

Singing a scale using numbers for the notes is very useful and we will do this a lot in later chapters. You can also play a scale yourself (and sing along) on a piano keyboard. Or use an online piano (see link in the resources section of the website).

So you see, depending on what note you start on, you end up with a different combination of black and white keys. In the key of C we only use the white keys on the piano. In the key of G, we use one black key. If you start on another note, you will find that you are using a different number of black keys. But in all cases, when we use this same pattern of half-steps and whole-steps (whole-whole-half-whole-whole-whole-half) it sounds "in tune." That is the diatonic scale.

Tip

If you are confused by the illustration on the previous page, here is the bottom line: "do (whole step) re (whole step) mi (half step) fa (whole step) so (whole step) la (whole step) ti (half step) do" ... and onward continuing up using the same pattern....

Non-Western Scales: Different cultures use different scales in their music, creating a different kind of feel to the sound of their music. Think of how Chinese music sounds different from Greek music, which sounds different from American folk music. Different genres of Western music such as Jazz, Blues or Avant-Garde also sometimes use different scales (made up of different patterns of whole-steps and half-steps). Some musical systems even have more notes than others. Arabic music, for instance, uses notes in its scale that Western music doesn't even have — the octave is subdivided differently than in the Western scale, into what we might think of as quarter steps (as opposed to just half and whole steps). It's a big world with many musical languages.

Key: There are two definitions of this word used in this book...

A "key" is the word for the part of the piano that you push down to sound a note.

A "key" is also the term to describe the scale you're singing or playing in. As I mentioned, you can start your diatonic scale on any note (always keeping the same interval pattern), but the scale will be higher or lower, and have a different name, depending on what note you start on. Whatever note you start your scale on is the "key" of your scale. If you start your scale on the C note, you're playing your scale in the key of C. You might say, "We're singing Frère Jacques in the "key of A," and that would mean that you're using notes from the scale that starts and ends with the A note.

Movable Scale: A movable scale refers to the fact that any given scale can start on any note (as we've just discussed), so it is movable up and down an instrument, or if sung, can be sung starting on any pitch (or in any key). If a song feels too high for you in the key of G, you can choose to sing it in a lower key that feels more comfortable for your voice. (Moving it this way is also called "transposing.") In other words, the song, and the scale in which it's sung, retains its shape and its tune, even if it is moved.

If you're singing by yourself or with other singers, without other instruments, you can just slide your song up or down to wherever it's comfortable for everyone to sing it. You don't need to worry about what the key you're singing in is called, or if it matches up with other instruments. It's only important that it feels good.

Fixed Scale: On the other hand, if you are singing with an instrument, you will need to coordinate with that instrument (or instrumentalist) so that you are both singing or playing in the same key; you are fixing the scale into a particular key. When you choose to sing a song in a specific key, you are singing in a fixed scale.

Sharps and Flats: Usage of the terms sharp and flat can vary depending on context.

Technically, "sharp" means a half step up the scale; "flat" means a half step down the scale.

On the piano, each of the black keys are called the sharps and flats and are named in relation to the white keys that they are next to. Because each black key is next to two different white keys, they can each have two names. So confusing! See the illustration below.

All the Note-Names Including the Sharps and Flats

Below is a piano keyboard showing the name of each note written on each key. Each black key has two names. (This illustration shows three octaves)

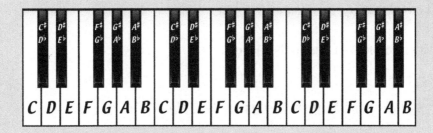

Just remember: Flat is a half step down, Sharp is a half-step up. In musical notation (the written language of music) the symbol for sharp looks like this: ♯, and the symbol for flat looks like this: ♭ .

Sometimes musicians use the words sharp and flat to refer to a place in the music where a sharp or flat occurs unexpectedly, and is an exception to the scale pattern. This usually gives the tune a little extra spice, or unexpected twist. In musical notation, this would be marked with the sharp or flat symbol (♯ or ♭) placed right next to the sharped or flatted note.

Sharp and flat can also be used as words of criticism or critique as in, "You're flat, Dude." "You're flat," means you're singing your song or note a little lower than intended or expected. "You're sharp" means you're a little too high.

Major and Minor Diatonic Scales: The major diatonic scale is the one we've been talking about so far.

The minor diatonic scale has a couple of important differences; the most significant for our purposes here is that the third note is flatted — it's a half-step lower than in the major scale.

Let's look at the intervals between just the first five notes of the major diatonic scale using the numbers of the notes:

"1 (whole-step) 2 (whole-step) 3 (half-step) 4 (whole step) 5"

Now, let's look at the minor diatonic scale.

"1 (whole-step) 2 (**half-step**) 3 *Flat* (**whole-step**) 4 (whole step) 5"

We have shifted the 3 note one half step down, thereby changing the intervals between it and both of the notes next to it.

Now, let's take a look at this on the piano ...

Major and Minor Scales in the Key of C (1st Five Notes)

Major Diatonic Scale in the Key of C

Minor Diatonic Scale in the Key of C

Have a listen:
Play track 17 to hear the difference between a major scale and a minor scale. 🔊

It's amazing that such a small shift can create such a very different sound.

Often people talk about the major scale as sounding happy and the minor scale as sounding sad or more soulful. Do you agree?

1, 3 and 5: Start counting up from the first note in any scale but skip some notes so that you're only playing the first, third and fifth notes (the 1, 3 and 5). Play track 18 to hear how this sounds. 🔊

These notes have a special harmonic relationship to each other and create a pleasing sound to our Western ear. (When you play them all at the same time it's called a chord.) Being able to identify the 1, 3 and 5 of the scale in the key you are singing in is a very useful tool, which we will use often as we proceed.

Root Note or Tonic Note: The first note in a given scale. (Referred to above, and frequently as we proceed, as the "1" note.) A song usually ends on the root note of the key in which it's sung. That's what gives you the satisfying sense of closure and the feeling that the song is over.

Bass, Tenor, Alto and Soprano: Terms referring to different harmony parts in a chorus or choir. Bass is the lowest, tenor is next lowest, then alto, and soprano is the highest. There are also other terms for the "in-betweens." Any one of these parts can be singing the melody while other parts sing the harmonies, but the melody is typically found in the tenor, alto or soprano lines, not down in the bass line.

Dissonance: When you play certain notes together and they seem to disagree. If I play a note along with the sharp of that note, let's say an A and an A#, I am creating a dissonance. It's a clashy sound. The vibrations create a feeling of choppiness.

Think of motorboats on a lake. If one motorboat follows directly in the path of another the waves they create will synch up and be in harmony with each other. If the two boats diverge, the waves they create will bump and splash and vibrate. That's more like dissonance.

Dissonance isn't bad; harmony isn't better. They just have different qualities. Don't be afraid of dissonance, because getting familiar with it will help you learn to sing on key, and also, in some contexts, dissonance can be very beautiful.

The Shruti Box: This could be your new best friend!

*The Shruti Box comes from India and was
created to be an accompaniment instrument
for other more complex instruments, including the voice.*

*It is hand-operated, bellows-powered, and very simple to play.
The Shruti provides a rich drone background to support
singing and musical exploration.*

Watch Video 10 to see and hear how I play and sing with my Shruti.

Chapter 14
Matching Pitch
& Singing with a Drone Note

So far we've approached singing from a free and exploratory perspective in which there is no such thing as right or wrong. Now we will make a shift into the world of measuring and comparison. The idea here is to remain in a place of non-judgement while working towards the specific goal of singing exactly the same note as you are hearing.

All the exercises in the previous chapters — assessing your singing strengths and challenges, exploring your voice with drones and sirening, and listening in new ways — are the first steps of learning to match pitch and sing in tune. So, you've already started!

The key to singing in tune is learning to recognize the *feeling* of matching a single note. Think about this: There are an infinite number of notes that you could be hitting when you try to match a note, so if you can do it even once, then you're not actually tone deaf, right? You are probably able to recognize when someone else is singing out of tune because it sounds wrong somehow, or because what you're hearing doesn't match up with what you were expecting to hear, but you may not yet be able to pinpoint why.

When learning to sing in tune, a whole song can be a lot to tackle at once because there are so many elements involved — the melody, the rhythm, and the words. Learning to match pitch while singing a song can also be hard because everything is happening so fast. So we'll begin by isolating the skill of singing the notes we hear, one at a time, and we will take it slow.

But first, let's figure out the best way for you to use this chapter. Check out the following three descriptions and, to the best of your ability, choose the one that most closely describes you. If you did the self-assessments in Chapter 7, refer to the notes at the end of Exercise 7.2 on page 75 to help you.

"To better hear the magic of an interval, sing along with a drone and listen to the universe of beats that occur as you slowly slide out of the unison and up to the half-step."
– Jim Oshinsky,
*   Return to Child;*
*   The Music For People*
*   Improvisor's Guide*

1. You are able to match a pitch quite easily, although you may have trouble keeping in tune throughout an entire song.

2. You have trouble matching a pitch, but recognize when you are off pitch, because something about what you're singing doesn't sound or feel right to you. You are also able to recognize when you are singing in tune.

3. You don't know when you're singing on or off pitch, and need feedback from someone else to recognize what's going on.

If choices #1 or #2 best describe you, then you will be able to use this chapter independently, with the help of the online audio tracks to strengthen your pitch-matching skills.

If #3 describes you best, go ahead and do this exercise but check in with a friend at some later time to get feedback on your perceptions about when you are and aren't matching the pitch. Over time you will become more and more independent, and able to assess by yourself when you are on pitch.

Ideally you'll get honest feedback from someone you consider supportive and encouraging, who is clear that they can recognize when two notes are the same. You can also use a pitch-matching app or website that gives visual feedback to tell you whether or not you're matching a note you're hearing. Visit the resource section of the website for a link. Although I think working with another person is preferable, this kind of technology can be helpful for some people, because it enables you to see, in privacy, when you are and aren't matching a pitch.

No matter how you answered the questions above it's time to start the next exercise.

Matching and Sliding with a Drone

A drone just means that one note is being held for a long time. Because this note doesn't change, the drone gives you the opportunity to sing with it and notice what you are doing in comparison to it. This is the most fundamental compare-and-contrast exercise you can do. It's good for beginners and it's also wonderful for experienced musicians, because it allows you to explore deeply all that happens when two notes occur in relation to each other: how they sound, how they vibrate in the air, and how they feel in your body. It sounds and feels different when you are singing the exact same note (and are in unison) as opposed to when you are singing a note that's very close (dissonance) or a different note that is a little further away. Exploring this vibrational movement is the essence of music making. For both experienced and beginning singers this can be profoundly moving and educational.

Notes sung in unison produce a feeling of smoothness because the sound waves have the same frequency; the sounds are in agreement with each other. The experience of sliding your voice slowly up and down, above and below the drone allows you to feel and hear this and to develop the ability to recognize when you are and aren't in unison.

Two notes that are sung very close together but not quite in unison might be called "out of tune" or "off-pitch" in some contexts, because they create a choppiness in the air caused by the sound waves being almost, but not quite, the same frequency. So if you do it in the middle of a song by accident, the effect probably won't be pleasing. But in the context of singing with a drone, this effect can be gorgeous. It's called dissonance, and if you pay attention you can literally feel the sound waves pulsing in the air. It's trippy and intense and transporting. Yummy.

So take the time to register the sensations in your whole body, and the vibrations in the air around you, as you sing with a drone in these exercises. This is something you can and should come back to frequently. A drone can be your backup band. It can support you in your vocal exploration. I know lots of accomplished musicians who do this exercise regularly and never stop learning new things from it.

Exercise 14.1: Matching a Drone Note
Track 19 (female) or Track 20 (male) 🔊))

On Track 19 you will hear me singing one long note. When I run out of breath, I take another and continue to sing that same note. You'll hear the same note three times and then you'll hear me switch to a different note and sing that three times. This pattern will continue with eight different notes in total. If you are male, go to Track 20 where you will hear a man's voice singing the pattern I just described; this will probably be easier for you to match.

Join in and do your best to sing the same note you're hearing. Take your time with this. Remember to tune into the sensations that are produced. One clue is that if we're on the same note, there will be a sensation of smoothness in the air and it may be hard to tell our voices apart. It may even feel as if we're making just one sound together. If you're not sure whether or not you're matching the note, this is the time to find a friend to tell you.

When you think you're done, do it a little more, or plan a time to come back and do it again, because you want this to sink in on many levels. You want to hear and feel the sameness of the notes. It might also help to close your eyes and visualize that sameness. Take this opportunity to enjoy the experience as completely as you can.

Savor the feeling. This is a perfect opportunity to use the mediation techniques we practiced in Chapters 10 and 11. In the long run, this exercise will help you learn to recognize when you're singing in tune with those around you.

After you've done this for a while, write any thoughts or observations here. What's easy about it? What's hard? How did it feel? What did you discover?

_____

_____

_____

_____

_____

_____

_____

_____

_____

_____

_____

_____

_____

Exercise 14.2: Moving Slightly Away from the Drone Note & Back
Track 21 (female) and/or Track 22 (male) ◀))

Tracks 21 and 22 are exactly like the tracks you used for the previous exercise (Tracks 19 and 20), except that at the beginning of each set you'll hear an example of two voices doing what you'll be doing in this exercise.

Start by matching the note like you did before, but this time, let your voice travel just a tiny bit away from the note and then back again. Return often to that home base note. Let the experience of unison (singing the same note) feel like home. So you start at home, you take a little trip, and then you return home again.

When you leave unison, move your voice slowly, noticing what happens when you're very close to the home note and how it changes when you are further away, and what it feels like to return again to the home note. It doesn't matter too much exactly where you go; just absorb the different sounds and sensations as you travel. Stick with it — don't do anything else just yet. When you think you're done, do it once or twice more.

When you are very close to the note but not right on it, you are creating dissonance, and that has a particular feel to it. How would you describe it?

Photo by Emma Kipp

Did you feel a choppiness in the air with dissonance, or a pulsing? Compare that sensation to the feeling of singing in unison. Any more thoughts?

Did you get a feeling of returning home to a familiar place when you got back to the drone note? Is unison starting to become something you can recognize? Any more thoughts?

Exercise 14.3: Improvising Freely with the Drone Note
Listen to Track 23 (female) and/or 24 (male) 🔊))

These will be exactly like tracks 19 and 20 from Exercise 14.1, except that at the beginning of each set of three drones, you will hear an example of what you'll be doing in this exercise.

Once again, start by trying to sing the note I'm singing (or that Ben is singing on Track 24). That's home base. Once you have a solid connection to this note, try gradually venturing further away in your exploration, but keep returning again periodically to the same note I'm singing. Try sliding up and down, above and below my note. While this may start off like an exercise, allow yourself to move into real exploration. Follow your voice wherever it wants to go. Please, *please*, do not worry about whether or not you sound "good" or "pretty." You are in the zone of NO-MISTAKES. You can't get this wrong.

There is a whole world of sound and vibration to experience, and I want you to notice as much of it as you can. Feel the smooth gliding sensation of unison, feel the choppy tension created in the air when our voices are close to each other, and notice the variety of things that happen when we're further apart — all the sometimes choppy, sometimes rich and gorgeous sounds. Let yourself sink in to it. Open your mind to hearing all of it as true, valid music. You thought you couldn't sing but here you are — this is your voice! Luxuriate in the beauty of your own voice. Indulge yourself! Express yourself!

When you feel finished, take some time to write about this experience. This may be the first time you've truly sung from your heart. What was it like?

Exercise 14.4: Droning and Sliding with a Friend, Step One:

Choose a friend who is confident in his or her ability to sing in tune. If nobody comes to mind, ask around. You may be surprised to discover that some of your coworkers or acquaintances are secret singers! This exercise is such a cool thing to do, and if you're both relaxed, your friend will probably enjoy it as much as you do.

Ask your friend to pick a note, any note, and sing it out for you to hear. Ask them to do what you heard me doing on the drone recording; ask them to sing a drone note over and over, taking a breath whenever they need to and then starting right up again on the same note. (You might want to play Tracks 19 and 20 for them ahead of time so they understand in advance what they're supposed to do. ◀))) Listen to your friend sing for a few moments and then join in on the same note (as in Track 5 ◀))) . Don't worry if it takes a little trial and error; take your time. When you are sure that you're on the same note as your friend (possibly with the help of their feedback) *glom* onto that note. That note is home.

> **Tip**
>
> If you are unable to match your friend's note, try this: You sing a note (anything that pops out is fine) and have your friend match your note, and then proceed with the instructions in the paragraph to the left, using that note. The important thing is that you and your friend are both singing the same note.

Sing the note out on the vowel sound of "ahhh" (as in "otter") in a long, steady drone. Don't worry about how well you're singing; you're just making a sound. Do your best not to waver, but don't worry if you do. It's not easy for everyone to hold a long steady note. You may find that it takes practice. Relax and refresh your breath any time you need to, returning each time to singing that same note. You and your friend are now both singing the drone part, as you heard me do in Track 2. ◀))

When you are ready for a change or if you are feeling fatigued, do it again with a new note or a new vowel sound like "ooooo" or "eeee."

Step Two — Hold the Note While Your Friend Slides:

When you are both pretty solid on a note, indicate to your friend that you are ready for them to begin moving around vocally while you continue to hold that note. Your friend will begin to play around, slowly moving higher and then back again to the note that you are still singing. (You can find examples of this on Tracks 21 and 22.) ◀)) Notice what happens as they move up and then back. Is it hard to stay on your note? Do you feel pulled up towards their note? Do you need to sing a little louder to hold your own? If you find it too difficult to sustain one long note you may want to skip right to Step Three, where your friend sings the drone and you get to be the person who moves around, and then come back to this part of the exercise at a later time.

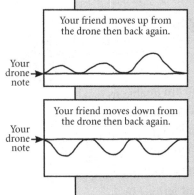

As your friend begins to pull away from your drone, do you feel the vibration in the air that indicates you are singing dissonant tones? If so, notice where you feel it. Is it in your face? In your chest? In your ears?

Now ask your friend to dip *below* the note you're singing. Have them start with you on the drone note and then slide slowly to a lower note and then slowly back up to your note. How is this different from when they went higher? Is it easier or harder to stick with your note?

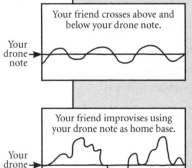

If you find it hard to tell when your friend is higher, lower or in unison with you, ask them to indicate with hand gestures; they can point up when they're higher, down when they're lower, or make a level gesture to indicate when they are in unison with you.

After you do this for a while, ask your friend to start on a note below the drone note you are singing. Then have them slide up very slowly, passing right through your note to a note above you. See if you can feel and hear the brief moment when their note is the same as yours as they travel up and down.

Now ask your friend to start improvising — just singing whatever feels most natural and interesting for them in relation to your one sustained drone note. (I've got examples of this for you on Tracks 23 and 24.) 🔊 Enjoy it, noticing how it feels and sounds.

Step Three — Switch it Around:

Now it's your turn — and you may actually find this to be easier than Step One, where it was your job to always stay on the same note, which is not as easy as it sounds! Pick a note, any comfortable note. Ask your friend to match it. This time your friend holds the drone, taking a breath whenever they need one but always returning to the same drone note. And it's your turn to try sliding above and below the drone note that they are singing. This note is "home"; notice how it feels to leave it and then to come back to it. As you do this for a while, with your friend's feedback, you'll find that you are becoming more adept at recognizing when you're in unison.

Use hand movements to indicate to your friend when you think you are above, below, and in unison with the note they're singing. Ask them to let you know if you're correct; they can give you a thumbs-up when you're right on, or point up or down with their index finger if you need to go higher or lower.

Try this with a variety of higher and lower drone notes as well.

How did you feel about droning and sliding with a friend?

Exercise 14.5: Improvising Freely with a Friend

While your friend holds a drone note for you, you will create your own music in the moment, the same way you did with the recording in Exercise 14.3. Move your voice up, down and all around as the spirit moves you. Try different shapes with your mouth (oooh, eeeeee, hey). Try closing your eyes and feel yourself sinking and rising, soaring and melting back into the sound of your friend's voice. Play with being louder and softer. Follow your voice as it expresses who you are and what you are feeling in the moment. This is your very own song in this one and only moment, and there is absolutely no way to get it wrong!

Your friend may feel inspired to change their note to connect more closely with your improvisation; ask them to follow their impulses. Now you are *really* making music with someone. I encourage you both to get into the beauty and power of this.

After you're finished, take a moment to write down some thoughts about this experience. How did it feel to do this exercise with a friend in comparison to doing it with a recording? Did you find the visual communication and eye contact to be helpful? Did it feel more powerful? Less powerful? Were there things about this experience that surprised you?

Great job! I hope you have enjoyed pitch matching and exploring your voice using a drone note. Not only have you now sung with a friend, but you've sung in harmony! How wonderful — congratulations!

Doing Exercises That Use a Drone Brings Multiple Benefits

1. Pitch-matching skills
You are becoming more familiar with the contrast between singing in unison and singing out of unison. To sing in tune you need to be able to recognize this difference; when you move away from the "home" note and back again you're practicing this most essential pitch-matching skill.

2. Voice control
You are sustaining a tone for an extended period, taking a breath and then picking it up again. This practice increases your ability to control your voice, both in terms of pitch and breath control. It also helps you to be able to return to a "home" note, another key skill for singing.

3. Using your voice intentionally and expressively
Improvising with a drone offers support while you explore the quality of your voice, use different pitches and volumes, and different mouth shapes. As you become more familiar with your unique vocal qualities you'll also become more able to use your voice in an intentional and expressive way.

4. Uncovering your musical creativity
Improvising with the support of a drone gives you an opportunity to discover what music and tunes are living inside of you. This kind of exploration unleashes your musical intuition and creativity.

5. Delving into harmony
Even though you're not singing an actual "song," you are experiencing what it's like to sing in harmony. These simple exercises — especially if this your first foray into the world of harmony — can be powerful. The sound, the sensation, the vibration, making music with other people: This is singing!

Chapter 15
Audiation

Have you ever had a song stuck in your head? Or listened to a familiar song that suddenly shut off in the middle, and felt the urge to finish the tune up yourself? This is audiation, the inner process of making music even when there is no actual sound being produced. It's the aural equivalent of visualization. It's the mental process that deciphers the patterns and structures in what we're hearing, thereby making it possible to recognize it as music instead of just hearing it all as random sound. In essence, audiation is musical thinking.

Audiation is a great tool to help you learn to sing in tune. It's not really something we need to think about most of the time, because to some degree it happens automatically. But when we're focusing on pitch-matching, it's very useful to engage audiation more actively. The act of musically visualizing what we want to sing helps all our singing apparatus get ready and makes it more likely for the sound that comes out to be the one we intended.

Here's how you do it:

"If I cannot fly, let me sing."
– Stephen Sondheim

Exercise 15.1: The Missing Note
Track 25 🔊)

Choose a song you are very familiar with, say "Row, Row, Row Your Boat," or "The Happy Birthday Song," or a simple song from your childhood like "Bah, Bah, Black Sheep" or the Alphabet Song (which share the same tune, by the way). Sing it out loud two or three times as best you can. Now sing it again but leave out the last note. If you can't sing well enough yet to do this, ask a friend to sing it, stopping before the last note, or listen to Track 25. Notice what happens.

How do you feel? You might have a sense of agitation, an actual craving to hear that last note. If you don't sing it, but rather spend a few moments noticing what's happening in your mind, you might find that you are actually finishing the song in your head; singing the last note silently. If you don't find yourself singing it silently in your head automatically, try doing it on purpose. That's audiating!

Exercise 15.2: The Power of Aural Imagination

To help you understand the power of audiation, try this. Do a few siren sounds, (see Exercise 10.3) swooping from a very high voice to a very low voice. Really imitate the sound of a fire engine with your voice. Now touch your throat so you can feel your larynx moving with your hand or your fingers as you sing the siren sound.

Next, with your hand still touching your throat, imagine vividly that you are sirening — do everything but let out the actual sound. Can you feel with your hand the motion of your larynx moving up and down? If so, you are experiencing what I mean when I say that the act of audiating sets us up for singing what we are imagining. It's actually putting your body into the right position for the activity.

Now, with your hand still on your throat, try to vividly imagine singing the sirening sound without making any motion in your larynx. For many people that's hard to do! Your imagination and your body are so closely linked that, even when you aren't singing, your body can't always help but do a significant part of the physical job of singing.

Tip

A singing game that uses audiation is B-I-N-G-O. With each verse the singer progressively leaves out more and more words, but audiates the missing words to keep track of their place in the song. At the end there are no words left at all, only claps to mark the spots where the words were. If you know this song and how it works, try singing it now for a quick illustration of audiation at work.

Go to Track 26 ◀)) to sing it with me!

Audiation is a natural process that happens without our being aware of it. By slowing down, we can learn to isolate and develop it so that it becomes a useful tool that will help us to become better at singing on pitch.

Include audiation in your menu of tools to help train yourself to sing what you intend to sing. If you are practicing a particular interval (we'll use the song Row, Row, Row Your Boat as an example) you might do this: Observe that the words "row, row, row" are all sung on the same note and that the word "your" is sung on a new and higher note. You can take a break from *singing* the "your" note and just *imagine* that you're singing that note. After doing this for a few moments, go back to singing that higher note again. You may find that you are more accurate this time. And of course, you can apply this technique to any notes in any song you are trying to sing.

Chapter 16
Singing Scales and Patterns

When you think "singer," the image may come to mind of someone standing near a piano and practicing scales. Singing scales, or versions of scales, is a classic "singer" thing to do. Although you never *need* to practice scales in order to sing, there are some good reasons for doing it.

Singing scales (or parts of scales) is a way of achieving three goals:

1. Stretching your vocal muscles to loosen up so you can sing high, low, loud and quiet — gaining comfortable access to your entire range of pitch and volume. Much the same way you would stretch your legs before a run.

2. Strengthening your muscles so you gain more stamina and resilience.

3. Refreshing your muscle memory and reminding your ear, brain and vocal apparatus of the intervals between the notes in the scale.

This chapter is mainly about the how-to of singing scales. If you want more information about what a scale is, and how various scales differ from each other, return to Chapter 13.

When I say "scale" here, I mean the diatonic scale. You are probably familiar with this type of scale even if you don't know it, because it's used in most of our classical, folk and popular music.

It is helpful to be familiar with the diatonic scale, because most of the songs you will learn will probably be composed of notes from this, or a closely related, scale. The diatonic scale that I'm referring to might be familiar to you as "Do Re Mi Fa So La Ti Do." If you've seen "The Sound of Music" you've heard the song that says, "Doe, a Deer ..." in which the lyrics illustrate the Do Re Mi sounds in relation to one another in a fun way.

"You've got to learn your instrument. Then, you practice, practice, practice. And then, when you finally get up there on the bandstand, forget all that and just wail."
– Charlie Parker

NOTE ...
Pages 154-156 recap material covered in Chapter 13. If you already understand this feel free to skip ahead to the section on page 156, called "Time to Sing a Scale."

I want to introduce you to three different ways of singing the scale, each of which will help you think about it in different, and useful, ways.

1. We can use the words Do, Re, Mi, Fa, So, La, Ti, Do.
2. We can count our way up the scale using numbers (1-2-3-4-5-6-7-8).
3. We can use the letter names of the notes (for example: C-D-E-F-G-A-B-C).

Whichever way we sing and think about the diatonic scale, there are several principals that always apply:

1. It is always made up of 8 notes, the last of which is always an octave above the first.
2. The last note of one octave is always the first note of the following octave.
3. There is a specific pattern of distance between each of the notes; it's this pattern that defines the scale as diatonic.

The pattern of intervals between the notes of the major diatonic scale is always this:

Do   Re   Mi   Fa   So   La   Ti   Do
1 <u>Whole-Step</u> 2 <u>Whole-Step</u> 3 <u>Half-Step</u> 4 <u>Whole-Step</u> 5 <u>Whole-Step</u> 6 <u>Whole-Step</u> 7 <u>Half-Step</u> 8

Some people say that there are seven notes in an octave and some say that there are eight. This is because there are seven different notes (1-2-3-4-5-6-7), with the eighth note tacked on at the end to give it a completed sound. That eighth note is the same as the first note, but an octave higher. When you get to note number eight you can stop with a satisfied, complete feeling, or you can use that note to start singing the scale again in the next octave up.

Here's a way to look at it using numbers:
If you were to sing two octaves in a row it would look like this:
1-2-3-4-5-6-7-(8 or 1)-2-3-4-5-6-7-8
Eight and one are the same, see?

Here's a way of looking at it using the system of words called "Solfege":
Do Re Me Fa So La Ti (Do) Re Me Fa So La Ti Do
The Do in the middle is both the last note of the first octave and the first note of the second octave.

Saying 1-2-3 and saying Do Re Me are two ways of saying exactly the same thing.

Go to Track 27 to hear what this sounds like and follow along with the piano keyboard in the illustration below.

Major Diatonic Scale in the Key of C — Two Octaves (Track 27) ◀))

Tip

Watch Video #11 ▶ to hear and see how this works.

Here you can see the Do-Re-Mi system and the number system and how they are different ways of thinking about the same thing. You can also see the names of the specific notes of the scale when fixed into the key of C.

Start with the C and count up on just the white keys to the C above; you will be playing notes of a diatonic scale in the key of C. Notice that the C note in the middle is both the 8 note of the first octave and the 1 note of the second octave.

That's a familiar sound, isn't it? This is the scale we'll be working with soon, though we'll often be singing just one small piece at a time.

We don't have to start on a C though, because the scale is *movable*, meaning it can be sung starting on any note. As long as the notes have the same relationship to each other (the same pattern of whole-steps and half-steps) you can pick any note to start and it will still be a diatonic scale. For example, if you start on a G note and follow this pattern up to the next G note, you will have played a diatonic scale in the key of G.

Tip

Notice that if you start on a note that is *not* a C, you will need to play one or more of the black keys to keep the pattern of whole and half-steps the same. You can find more detail on this back in Chapter 13.

In the illustration below you can see how a diatonic scale looks on a piano, in keys other than C. Remember, a half step is always the next key away; a whole step is always 2 keys away. Use the illustration to count these out and you will see that even though at first glance these scales look different, they always adhere to the same pattern:

1 Whole-Step 2 Whole-Step 3 Half-Step 4 Whole-Step 5 Whole-Step 6 Whole-Step 7 Half-Step 8

Go to Track 28 and follow along with the illustration. 🔊

Tip

Watch Video #12 ▶
to hear and see how this works.

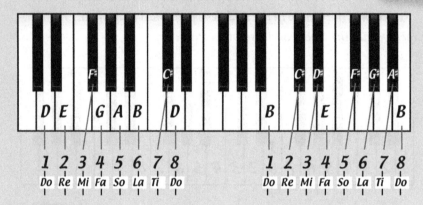

Major Diatonic Scale in the Keys of D and B. (Track 28) 🔊

Count out the whole-steps and half-steps.

Understanding this bit of theory might help you to learn to sing scales especially if you're a cognitive or visual learner. It's good information to have. But what's most important, however you do it, is to get really comfortable over time singing notes in the diatonic scale, at first bit by bit and perhaps eventually in its entirety, because being able to sing these intervals will help you when you're singing songs.

Let's Do It!

Now, you may say, "Well, that's just fine, but I can *see* the notes on the piano. I can't see the notes in my voice. How do I know how to sing the correct notes?"

We will take it slowly, starting with just small chunks of the scale. Reach into your bag of tricks — read the reminders on the next page. Use your pitch matching techniques from Chapter 14. Sing along with the tracks in the upcoming exercises. After a while you'll be able to tell when you're off and when you're nailing it, and you'll be able to do it more easily because all your practice and repetition has helped you build muscle memory.

When learning the scale patterns in this chapter, remember to use your resources! Here are a few that are particularly helpful:

• The piano, or illustration of the piano, can help you understand how the notes of the pattern you are practicing relate to each other.

• You can use your hand to mark out the notes of the pattern you are singing in the air, adding *kinetic* and *visual* support to the mix. (See the illustration on the right side of this page.) ⟶

• Use the recordings to practice matching the pitches in the patterns. Now that you've experienced what it sounds and feels like to match one pitch at a time, you'll find that you're able to *listen* to the different notes in these patterns in a deeper way. This will help you as you learn each of these patterns as separate little tunes.

You understand it, you can visualize it, you can move your body to it, you can hear it, you can feel it. You can recognize to some extent when you're doing it correctly. You can get feedback from a friend.

You are ready to give it a try!

Below are several exercises that may come to you easily, or that you may need to repeat over and over before you feel confident. In the exercise tracks I sing either the whole scale, or bits and pieces of the scale, in a variety of combinations. After you've worked on your own for awhile, you might want to check in with a friend for feedback about how accurate you are becoming.

> **Tip**
>
> Look at this vertical rendition of the scale.
>
> Read the names and numbers of the notes out loud, starting at the bottom.
>
> Touch each letter or number as you sing it for a little extra kinetic support!
>
> A—8
> G—7
> F—6
> E—5
> D—4
> C—3
> B—2
> A—8 or 1
> G—7
> F—6
> E—5
> D—4
> C—3
> B—2
> A—1

Exercises 16.1 - 16.8: Major Scale Pattern Exercises
(Tracks 29-36 with female voice, Tracks 29b-36b with male voice) 🔊

Approach these in a variety of ways: Sing in unison with me, or sing in call-and-response with me (I go, you go). Pause the track while you sing and then play it back again with me to check your accuracy. Do these in order or skip around to what is most appealing or useful. Enjoy it!

Exercise 16.1: 1-2-3-4-5-6-7-8 (Track 29 female, Track 29b male) 🔊
This is the whole diatonic scale. If you can't sing along with it yet, just listen to it a few times so it sinks in subliminally, and then come back to it after you've done the following exercises, which use smaller pieces of the scale.

Exercise 16.2: 1-2, 1-2, 1-2 (Tracks 30 & 30b) 🔊 Notice how you can slide from note to note, or jump from note to note.

Exercise 16.3: 1-2-3, 3-2-1 (Tracks 31 & 31b) 🔊 Sink into the sound of each note and get familiar with the specific relationship between these notes. Enjoy the feeling of returning home to the 1 note. And again, notice the different ways you can transition from one note to another.

Exercise 16.4: 1-2-3-4-5, 5-4-3-2-1 (Tracks 32 & 32b) 🔊 Wheee! Take it slow though! Continue to focus on pitch-matching with each note, and feeling the "shape" of this little tune as a whole. It can be tricky to stay in tune with this many notes!

Photo by Judith (©Judepics).
Singing Gorkhas in Darjeeling, October 2008

Exercise 16.5: 1-3-5, 5-3-1 (Tracks 33 & 33b) 🔊

Skipping 2 and 4, sing just the 1, 3 and 5. The 1, 3 and 5 have a nice harmonious relationship to each other. Together they make a major chord. Later, if you want to learn to sing harmony, it will be extremely useful to have memorized the feeling of these notes in relation to each other because when you sing one of these notes at the same time as someone else sings another one of them, together you'll be singing a harmonious chord with your voices. Knowing how to find this progression with your voice is also very helpful when you are learning and singing songs; understanding and having muscle memory of the 1-3-5 notes gives you access to clues about the notes in your songs.

Exercise 16.6: 1-3-5-8 (Tracks 34 & 34b) 🔊

Like the above exercise, but now you're also jumping up to the 8 (which is the same note as the 1, remember? The 1 and 8 are the same note but an octave apart!).

Exercise 16.7: 1-3-5-8, 8-5-3-1 (Tracks 35 & 35b) 🔊

Singing the 1-3-5-8 notes forward and backward. You da bomb. This one's great for stretching and warming up your voice, and for getting your voice and brain tuned up before you start singing. Choral groups use this as a warm-up all the time!

Exercise 16.8: I Can Sing High High High and Other Variations With Words (Tracks 36 & 36b) 🔊

These are some variations on scale exercises that are used by many singers, and in choral warm-ups. They use the 1, 3, 5, & 8 (and sometimes an extra 8 or two) forwards and backwards, and with words. Try singing "I can Sing High-High-High I Can Sing Low" or "Reinforced Toe Pantyhose" or "I Am Not Scared Anymore!" or anything else that strikes your fancy. Try starting the pattern on a low note, and then repeating it over and over, moving the starting note a little higher each time.

The Minor Diatonic Scale

The minor diatonic scale has a whole different feel, but surprisingly, it's just the shifting of one or two notes that creates this difference. In the next exercise you'll listen and try it yourself. It's really cool!

Exercise 16.9: Lowering the Third for a Minor Scale
(Tracks 37 with a female voice & 37b with male voice) 🔊

So far you've been singing the major diatonic scale; now you will be singing the minor diatonic scale. The only thing we'll do differently is to sing the 3 note a half-step lower than in the major scale.

Listen to Tracks 37 and 37b to hear the 1-3-5 notes sung in both major and minor scales. That one change creates a profoundly different sound and feel, doesn't it?

Listen carefully to compare which notes are the same and which are different. Then sing along so that you can feel the difference and begin to build it into your muscle memory. It's a lot of fun to sing songs and to improvise in a minor scale. It can be very soulful.

Have fun with this! Practice singing scale patterns, as often as you want. Remember, even many advanced singers often sing scales or parts of scales to get warmed up and re-tune their ear and sense of pitch in preparation for singing, much the way a runner gets ready by stretching before going for a run. It helps us reconnect what we hear to what comes out of our mouth! If done mindfully, singing scale patterns can also help us reconnect to our love of singing and get us into the zone.

For beginners, practicing patterns like these is also a way of building muscle memory, and gaining control of your voice so it's easier to find the notes you are looking for and to sing what you intend.

Photo by Bert Salwen, circa 1955.
Pete Seeger and Fred Hellerman, members of the influential singing group,
The Weavers. My dad took this photo of them playing and singing at a
house concert in the 1950s.

When I was a child I learned many, many songs from these and other
musicians from the folk music scene of the 1950s and 60s.
Before I was born, my parents, who were social justice activists,
hung out with some of these musicians.

During my childhood their records and songs were around our house
and were the foundation of my love of singing.

Chapter 17
How to Approach a Song

In this chapter we'll walk through a few different approaches to learning the melody (or tune) of a song. The first approach is more analytical and will take you along step by step, using your understanding of the scale and the 1-3-5-8 note relationships to work with the song, "Row, Row, Row Your Boat." Once you've practiced these techniques with this song, you'll be able to apply them to other songs that you want to sing. If it's more than you can make sense of at this stage, just read through it and move on to the rest of the chapter. You'll be absorbing the information on a subconscious level and can return to it whenever you're ready.

The second approach is more intuitive and focuses on visualizing the shape of a song, feeling the relationship of the notes in your body, and learning by ear using lots of repetition.

Ideally, over time you will be able to use both of these approaches, moving back and forth between them in whatever way feels best to you.

The Analytic Approach:
Your Song in Relation to the 1-3-5

Do you remember how in the last chapter I made a big deal about the 1, 3 and 5 of the scale? I mentioned that being able to sing those notes of the scale in any key would come in handy. We'll be working with this now.

This is also the time to bring in all the learning style tools you discovered in Chapter 6, pages 64-67. Refer to those pages for helpful ideas about working creatively with a variety of learning styles including kinetic (using your hands and your body), visual (charting or notating what you're singing), and cognitive (understanding concepts about what you're singing). When we approach a song, we want to use everything we have in our bag of tricks!

Row, Row, Row Your Boat in the Key of C

Our first song will be "Row, Row, Row Your Boat," because it's easy to analyze its relationship to the 1, 3 and 5 notes; we'll use the key of C so that when we refer to the keyboard, we can use all white notes.

"Singing is like holding hands,
Voices are like fingers
 intertwined,
Sometimes you give
 a friendly squeeze,
Sometimes a caress,
Sometimes you
 even pinch each other.
Singing is an act of faith,
Trusting one another
 to be there
In moments of fear
When someone else's voice
 becomes your net;
In moments of hope
When someone else's dreams
 Reinforce yours
 And give you courage,
In moments of emptiness
 When comradeship
 can make you full.
To have held to this faith
 for 20 years is no small feat.
But such is love."
– Mary Travers, June 1, 1982,
 from the jacket of the record
 "Such is Love"
 by Peter, Paul and Mary

Because we'll be working in the key of C, the root note (the note that gives the song a feeling of resolution and the note that many songs end on, including this one) will be a ... that's right ... a C!

To review: Remember that the scale is made up of seven notes plus the 8 (which is also the 1 of the next octave up). We have several ways to refer to the notes in our C scale; all of the following are different ways of saying exactly the same thing:

Do Re Mi Fa So La Ti Do
1-2-3-4-5-6-7-8
C D E F G A B C (since we're in the key of C)

For the following exercise, listen to Track 38 and follow along using the illustration below; you can also refer to a real piano or online keyboard if you have one available. (The key of C only uses white notes, so while you're following along just stay on the white notes!)

This will help you conceptualize the ideas we're working with, and learning to work with a keyboard will be helpful if you ever want to use a piano while doing your singing exercises in the future.

Exercise 17.1: Learning to Sing Row, Row, Row Your Boat
Track 38 Note: After you've gone through Track 38 following along with the illustration, try listening and singing with Tracks 38b and/or 38c (male and female in the key of G), and see where your voice is most comfortable.

Step 1: Go to Track 38 and listen to the C note I'm singing and playing there. Find the C note in the illustration below.

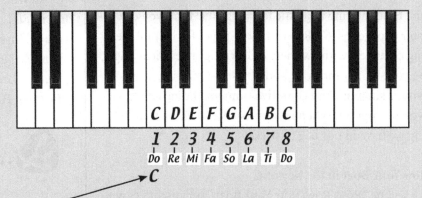

Sing this C note for a minute. Get to know it. This is your new home while we are working on this song.

Step 2: Next, sing along with me. We will sing the C scale. Sing it saying the names of the notes: C-D-E-F-G-A-B-C. Sing it saying 1-2-3-4-5-6-7-8. Sing it saying do-re-mi-fa-so-la-ti-do. Point to the notes that you are singing on the illustration (previous page) as you sing them. Refer back to audio tracks as much as you need to.

Step 3: Now sing "1-2-3-4-5" and "5-4-3-2-1" pointing to the notes while you sing them.

Step 4: Next, sing "1-3-5" and "5-3-1." Repeat ad nauseam. Point to the notes while you sing them.

Step 5: Now listen to and sing along with me. On the pitch of the 1 (the C, since we're in the key of C), sing the word "Row" along with the recording. Sing it three times on that exact same note in groups of three. Do it a bunch of times:

"Row, Row, Row. Row, Row, Row. Row, Row, Row." Sing it until you're confident that you're singing the same note each time.

Step 6: Next, sing just the first three notes of the C scale using the words, "one, two three." "1-2-3. 1-2-3. 1-2-3."

Step 7: Now sing: "One, One, One Two Three" and then, on the same notes, sing "Row, Row, Row Your Boat." Get it? As you sing the words to the song, visualize the notes in the scale. See how they relate to each other like steps in a staircase.

Step 8: Check this out: If we mark out all the notes in the song this way, it looks like this:
1-1-1-2-3
3-2-3-4-5
8-8-8-5-5-5-3-3-3-1-1-1
5-4-3-2-1

Here are the numbers of the notes, along with the words of the song:
(Try singing along!)

1   1   1   2   3
row row row your boat
 3   2   3   4   5
gent-ly down the stream
 8   8   8 5   5 5 3   3 3 1   1 1
mer - ri - ly, mer - ri - ly, mer - ri - ly, mer - ri - ly
 5   4   3   2   1
life is but a dream

So you're singing a song, and you're understanding how the notes relate to each other, right?! Congratulations!

Notice how you can use observations about this song to create "markers" to help you learn it:

• The 1, 3, 5 and 8 notes of the scale occur frequently in this song. Because we have practiced singing these intervals before (in Chapter 16) we have developed some understanding and muscle memory around them, so we may be able to find these notes more easily now.

• The phrases in this song all start and end on the 1, 3 or 5 (remember, the 8 is also a 1, just an octave higher). See if knowing this makes it easier to find these notes with your voice.

• The reason the song sounds finished at the end is because it ends on the 1 (in this case the C, which is the root note of the C scale). Because this song also *starts* on the 1, it is easy to find your starting place if you want to sing the song again — just start on the same note you finished on.

• The highest note in the whole song is on the first occasion of the word "merrily." All three syllables of the word "mer-ri-ly" are sung on the 8, which is an octave above the 1, where the song started.

Tip

This is a perfect time to use your learning style techniques!

They will help you make cognitive, visual and kinetic connections.

• Move your hands up and down to mark the steps out in the air.

• Draw a picture of the ups and downs and patterns in this song.

• Tune into the feeling of the movement in your throat and the vibrations in your chest.

Tune into whatever clues and methods help you the most. It's not cheating – this is how it's done!

Now you have some concepts to better understand the structure of this song. Rather than having "merrily" be just some mysterious distant high note you're trying to throw a dart at, you now have a logical target. You know that it's the high C (the 8) and an octave above the first note of the song. Because you've been practicing singing the 1-3-5-8 in Chapter 16, you are familiar with the feeling and sound of the jump from the 5 to the 8, so that leap from "stream" to "merrily" is a familiar interval.

What do you notice about the third line of this song? It's moving down steadily, isn't it? In four sets of three notes. "8-8-8, 5-5-5, 3-3-3, 1-1-1". Each "merrily" is made up of three syllables, each sung on exactly the same note. And there's a real pattern in how they descend from that first high merrily to the last one that's sung on the root note. If you've gotten comfortable singing the 1, 3, 5, 8, then you won't have too hard a time finding these descending merrilys — it's just the 1-3-5-8 backwards. 888-555-333-111, life is but a dream! Yes! We're ready for the last line, life is but a dream. 5-4-3-2-1. Hurray!

Do you see that you can use your knowledge of the scale, and particularly of the 1-3-5-8 relationships, to help you understand any song?

Here are questions you can ask as you approach any new song:

1. What note does the song END on, and is it the "1," or root note, of my song?
Listen to the song and hum along with the very last note; that will often be the "1" of the scale that your song is in — very handy! Knowing which note is the 1 gives you a baseline with which to compare all the other notes in the song.

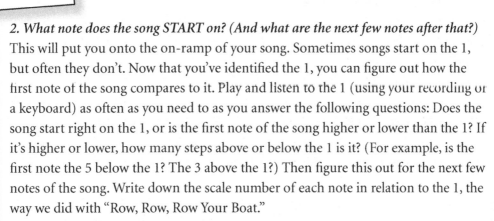

Photo by James Fulker/DFID.

If the last note is *not* the 1, the big question is, where *does* the 1 note show up? Learning how to find and sing the 1 of a song will definitely hone both your listening and pitch-matching skills, and at first you may need someone to help you with this. Once you've identified that note, it's helpful to play it on a keyboard or make a recording of it so you can keep listening to just that note as you continue to work on the song. Return to it often and/or sustain it long enough to compare it to some of the other notes in the song.

> **Tip**
>
> Most popular songs in Western music end on the "1," which gives them a resolved, finished feeling. A clue that a song does *not* end on the "1" is that it tends to leave you with a less resolved feeling. "The Song that Never Ends," for example, feels so unfinished that you want to circle back and sing it again.

2. What note does the song START on? (And what are the next few notes after that?)
This will put you onto the on-ramp of your song. Sometimes songs start on the 1, but often they don't. Now that you've identified the 1, you can figure out how the first note of the song compares to it. Play and listen to the 1 (using your recording or a keyboard) as often as you need to as you answer the following questions: Does the song start right on the 1, or is the first note of the song higher or lower than the 1? If it's higher or lower, how many steps above or below the 1 is it? (For example, is the first note the 5 below the 1? The 3 above the 1?) Then figure this out for the next few notes of the song. Write down the scale number of each note in relation to the 1, the way we did with "Row, Row, Row Your Boat."

Here's an example of how I've used this technique: I used to repeatedly mix up the tune of "This Land is Your Land," by Woody Guthrie, with the tune of "You Are My Sunshine," (folkie that I am). I'd start to sing "This Land is Your Land," only to find that I was lost in the middle. Something just wasn't right — I could tell that I was singing the wrong notes. So I sat down and analyzed the situation using this method, and saw my mistake. I realized that the first four notes of "This Land is Your Land" are 1-2-3-4. This gave me a sure-fire way to grab on to the tune. I realized that "You Are My Sunshine" starts on the low 5 (the 5 below the 1), and that my mistake had been to start singing "This Land is Your Land" on that low 5 — that was why I was getting lost — my first few notes were wrong. Using the fact that I was getting confused as a signal to myself to stop and do a little analysis helped me clear up my confusion. Now, because I understand how the first line of each tune works, and how they're different from each other, I don't have trouble with them anymore. I have a little mental note about each song that helps me remember the beginning, and once I'm in, I'm all set to go. You can do this, too!

3. What is the highest note of the song?

What word (or words, or parts of words) in the song are the highest? Knowing this is handy because it helps you to visualize the "shape" of the song.

If you are having trouble singing that highest note accurately, it can help to identify that high note in relation to the root note (the 1) of the song. One way to do this is to listen to the song and wait for the highest note to come around, and then catch it! Match it with your own voice and then count up to that note from the 1, to figure out exactly what that highest note is. Using a piano keyboard can be really helpful with this.

4. What is the lowest note?

Do the same thing as above, but with the lowest note of the song.

5. Where do the 1, 3 and 5 notes show up?

If you are having trouble gaining mastery of your song it can help to identify other landmarks in addition to the highest and lowest notes. Figuring out if and where the 1, 3 and 5 notes occur can be a great way of getting to know your song better and getting a solid sense of how the notes relate to each other. Find the root note, sing (or play on a keyboard) the 3, and then hold on to it while you're listening to the song and see if you can tell when the singer is singing your note. Do the same thing with the 1 and the 5. *Just a heads up that this can be a little tricky — if this feels too difficult don't be discouraged. This might be something you'll do further down the line.*

6. Are there patterns, or bits of the song that repeat themselves?

Perhaps the first line of a song has the exact same tune as the third line, or maybe the last three lines of the chorus has the same tune as the verses. This is a wonderful thing to recognize because if so, there's that much less to learn — you've already learned it!

These are the kinds observations and notes you can make about any song you want to learn. Using this analytic approach is the best way for some people to approach a song.

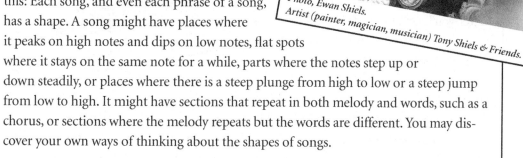

*Photo, Ewan Shiels.
Artist (painter, magician, musician) Tony Shiels & Friends.*

The More Intuitive Method

Another way of approaching a song involves less thinking and more feeling and visualizing. As you do the activities that follow, think about this: Each song, and even each phrase of a song, has a shape. A song might have places where it peaks on high notes and dips on low notes, flat spots where it stays on the same note for a while, parts where the notes step up or down steadily, or places where there is a steep plunge from high to low or a steep jump from low to high. It might have sections that repeat in both melody and words, such as a chorus, or sections where the melody repeats but the words are different. You may discover your own ways of thinking about the shapes of songs.

Understand the shape of your song.
Visualize the shape of your song as you listen to it. Start by simply closing your eyes as you listen to the song to get a visceral sense of the shape of it.

Try drawing your impression of the shape of your song on a piece of paper. Listen again and make circles around all the parts that seem to repeat. If there are parts that seem to repeat but include little exceptions, put an asterisk or a mark at about the place in the circle where the exceptions occur. Go back again later and notice what's happening in those exceptions.

Print out the lyrics of your song and make notes all over them.
Create your own code to help you understand the shape of the song in the ways we discussed above; make marks (dashes, arrows, wiggles, slopes, etc.) to show where there are chunks that repeat, where it's trending up or down, staying on the same note for a bunch of syllables, and exclamation points to show if there are parts of the song that surprise you! This is your language to use as an aid in learning the song; don't worry about whether it will make sense to other people or not — just do what works best for you. If you read music, you have a head start here, since sheet music is essentially an illustration showing where the notes of a song go up and down as it moves through time. Feel free to mark up your sheet music in ways that help you.

*Move your hands in the air, or move
your whole body, to show the shape
of the song.*

Play the song and as you listen,
illustrate the ups and downs of the notes
with movements that feel like they match
what you're hearing. Don't worry too
much about whether you're right or
wrong because the more you do this the
better you'll get at it. Just do your best
to connect physically with the shape of
the melody of your song.

Old postcard from Naples, Italy. Boy singing & old man playing.

Start with your favorite part.
Instead of starting at the beginning of the song, zero in on the part that attracts you
the most and work on that part first. Then expand outward from there. When you like
what you're working on it helps you to get a strong foothold, and that's a good way to
start!

Use call and response.
Create a call and response experience for yourself using short phrases of your song.
Play a recording and listen to the whole song. Then, listen to it again, but pause the
recording after just a short phrase. Now sing just that short phrase. Listen again, sing
it again; listen, sing; listen, sing. Compare; contrast. Once you've mastered that phrase,
move on to the next. Once you've got that one, try putting the two together. Keep
referring back to the recording to be sure you've got it right. Continue this way, phrase
by phrase, until you've mastered the whole song.

Use audiation.
Pause a recording of your song mid-phrase and try finishing the phrase yourself using
audiation (just *thinking* the music instead of actually singing — see page 151 for details).
Then listen to the second part of the phrase and see if it matches up with what you
just audiated. Now replay the phrase, and again pause it in the middle, but this time
actually sing the second part of the phrase. Compare what you sang, to what you
heard in the recording. Repeat, continually fine-tuning. Audiating helps train your
brain to process what you're hearing so that you can sing it more accurately.

What is apparent from this chapter is that learning a song requires a lot of repetition
and focus! This is true for experienced musicians and singers, but even more so for

new singers. This is because not only are you learning the particular song that you're working on, you are also *learning how to learn a song.* You are engaging your ear and your voice in very new ways, and this process requires a lot of practice and patience.

Take breaks whenever you feel the need, and don't let yourself get too frustrated. Sometimes it helps to sleep on it and come back to it the next day. Always build on your successes; when something works, do more of it and use it as a core to come back to. Then try adding other techniques to continually expand on your successes.

A Few Additional Pieces of Advice

Choose songs that are fairly simple.
While you're starting out, avoid songs that have great big interval jumps, or have a lot of notes that feel unpredictable or confusing. Focus on songs that make sense to you, so that you can understand the relationships between the notes on various levels (cognitive, kinetic, visual, auditory). However, there are exceptions to every rule: If you're drawn towards a more complicated song — and it comes easily to you — go for it anyway. Make it yours!

Sing your song in a key that is comfortable for you.
Use trial and error to be sure that whatever note you start on doesn't put you in a position where the high notes are too high or the low notes are too low.

Choose songs that don't have too wide a range for your voice.
Some songs have a wide range, meaning that the lowest note is far away from the highest note. If the notes are too far apart you may feel physically uncomfortable singing the highest or lowest notes. As a beginner it's better to choose songs that have a range that is comfortable for you; you'll become better at choosing after some trial and error. Later on you can work on expanding your vocal range, if you want to.

Choose songs that touch you.
Learning a new song can be a lot of work. Most of the time, it shouldn't feel like an exercise. It should feel like a joy. Working with songs you like, that speak to you and feel good will make the work feel worth it.

Or, choose songs that motivate you for some other worthwhile reason.
Perhaps you don't love a song, but still want to learn it for a specific occasion (you know that your sister will be asking everyone to sing it at her wedding, or you want to learn it for a sing-along at your kid's school). Even if you don't love the song, stay in touch with why you want to learn it, and picture yourself succeeding. Keep your excitement about the end game in your mind and let that keep you connected with the love!

Photo by Angela Sevin.
In African music, singing and dancing are often considered inseparable —
two parts of the same activity. In fact, in some places they are described
with the same terminology; a dance and the music used
to accompany it often have the same name.

Chapter 18
Get the Rhythm in Your Body

Another aspect of singing a song, besides learning the melody, is keeping the rhythm. This means both keeping the steady underlying rhythm, which I will also refer to as the pulse, beat, or heartbeat, of the song, and having a sense of how the song is structured in time so that you can know when to start singing and when to pause.

In this chapter you'll learn to feel the pulse of a song, and then, in the next chapter, we'll analyze how the beats are grouped and emphasized in any given song, and how that creates a structure that you can learn to understand.

Refer back to Chapter 7 for a quick check-in on the Self-Reflections you made of your rhythmic abilities. If rhythm comes quite naturally to you, you may not want to analyze how it works; feel free to skip this chapter and the next. If it ain't broke, don't fix it!

If you're not so sure, read on ...

Feeling the Heartbeat

Almost any song you hear or sing has a beat. The beat is the underlying pulse; it's what you'll most likely find yourself tapping your foot to. It's sometimes called the heartbeat of the song because it plays an analogous role in the life of a song to the role of our heartbeat in our life — it's continuous and life-sustaining. It feels natural. Connecting to the pulse of the song in both mind and body connects you to the whole song and will help you to sing it more confidently.

> **When it comes to RHYTHM, your body is smarter than your mind.**

> *"Our biological rhythms are the symphony of the cosmos, music embedded deep within us to which we dance, even when we can't name the tune."*
> – Deepak Chopra

Exercise 18.1: Feel the Heartbeat, Find the Cues

Play a recording of a song you like that has a strong rhythm. As you tune into the feel of it, notice the way the rhythm of the song makes your body want to move. Some songs have multiple rhythms playing at the same time — find the one that feels most natural. You might find yourself tapping your foot, tapping your leg with your hand, clapping, snapping your fingers, or getting up to walk or dance in time to the song. Whatever you do is fine — keep doing it!

What you're doing, even if you don't realize it, is marking the rhythm of the song with the movements of your body. As you continue, I want you to notice what you are feeling, hearing, seeing and thinking, in that order. These are all ways that your body has of absorbing and processing the steady pulse of this song. This exercise gives you the opportunity to become conscious of each one separately.

FEELING:
Notice the physical sensations of your rhythmic tapping or clapping;
feel the vibrations of the music in the air.

HEARING:
Notice any sounds that you are making. Listen to the sound of your clap, or your snap, or your tap and pay attention to how they are connecting with the sound of the music.

SEEING:
Watch your feet as they tap, your hands as they clap or your fingers as they snap. Consciously use your eyes to notice these visual markers of the beat. Later, when you're singing with other people you may find it helpful to use visual cues as a way of checking in to be sure you're in rhythm with the song and with everyone else.

THINKING:
Ask yourself questions and answer them.
- What sounds are cueing me in to rhythm — what input am I receiving that tells me when to clap, snap, tap or move my body? Drumbeats? The strums of a guitar? The emphasis on certain syllables sung by the vocalist?
- Is the energy of the beat relaxed, angry or excited? Is it fast? Is it slow?
- How does the rhythm speak to me? What do I notice about this?

Write down some of your observations here ...

Because you've consciously registered all of these channels through which your body takes in and processes rhythm, you can turn your attention to any of these channels whenever you need them. If you're feeling a little lost in a song or confused about its rhythm, you can tap your foot, clap your hands, shift your weight back and forth, get up and walk around while you're singing and feel the rhythm in your steps. Pop these techniques into your bag of tricks. You'll find them especially handy when you're singing with other people or an instrument.

I have always been a little more melodically inclined than rhythmically inclined. Recently the band I sing with decided to work on "Angel From Montgomery," by John Prine. I thought I knew that song because I'd been singing it for years. I knew all the lyrics, and the tune, but I'd been singing it by myself, unaccompanied. Because I didn't have to match my timing with anyone else (or any instruments) I didn't realize that I was using my own personal timing. I was stretching out phrases here and there to match my sense of the meaning of the song. That is a *fine* way to sing a song, unless you want to sing it with other people. So, to sing it with my band, I needed to relearn this song and break the habits I'd developed around its timing.

I counted, I stomped my feet to the beat, I made notes all over a page of the lyrics. All of that helped, but not enough. When I sang with the band I was still coming in late in some places and early in others. Finally, I thought to keep my eyes on the hand of the guitarist as I sang. I realized that he was changing chords in a specific way at the beginning of each verse, and that if I watched his hands for that specific movement, it could be my cue. He switches chords, and boom, I come in on the next beat. That visual cue worked for me. Now, after singing it many times using that cue, I have internalized the rhythm and can come in at the right moment without it. Now, I feel it in my body and I hear it.

Next, while listening to music, try just letting yourself go with it. In the next exercise you will keep feeling, listening and seeing, but you'll let the thinking go. The main idea here is, "When it comes to rhythm, my body is smarter than my brain."

Exercise 18.2: Let Your Body Take the Lead

Pick out a song you like. It can be the same song you used in the last exercise or a different one. Make sure you choose one that has a compelling rhythm and that grabs you!

Start off not moving at all. Just feel how the music makes you *want* to move. But resist! Listen in stillness, and just let the beat of the song sink in. Next, allow yourself to move to the beat of the song using only your torso. This might mean that you are just rocking back and forth a little bit, or it could mean that you are doing the twist! Once you feel the rhythm strongly in your core, allow your movements to extend out towards your extremities. You can bend your knees and bounce and swing your arms. Now, finally, go ahead and clap, tap, snap, etc. Bang on the furniture or jam with some pots and pans if you want. Starting your rhythmic movements from the core this way helps you to build a strong relationship with the beat of the song; the song becomes part of you.

Whether marking the beat of a song with your body is tricky for you or it comes naturally, this is the most fundamental way to make a connection to the beat of a song, so it's worth practicing. You might just think of it as dancing. And this may be all you need to do! Trust your body and let it take the lead!

If It's Not Broke, Don't Fix it

Again, I want to say that further analysis may not be necessary or helpful to you at this stage. If you find that you are singing the verses or phrases of songs at the same time as the people around you, or are synced up with the recording you're singing with, then don't worry about it. You might have this aspect of singing mastered already.

If you're like me, whose husband used to interrupt me mid-song with, "You missed a beat," and "You came in late there," then you might find it helpful to read on and work with some of the handy-dandy tips in the next chapter.

Chapter 19
Get the Rhythm in Your Song

If after getting the rhythm in your body you are still confused about the timing of your song, then counting the beats in your song is the next step. Counting out the beats is a way of keeping track of what is happening as a song moves through time. It's a way of understanding the song's structure and learning to start and stop singing at the right time. "It's been a hard day's night, and I've been working like a dog." You may have heard this Beatles song enough times to just naturally feel that there's a pause after "night" and to come in with "... and I've been" at just the right time, and if so, that's great — just sing the song! But if you feel awkward or unsure about where the stops and starts are, learning to count out the beats will help.

Here's how it works:

You figure out what you consider to be the first strong beat of the song (the first beat to have an obvious emphasis) and start counting from there. Sometimes it's easy to tell where to start, but sometimes it takes a little detective work — and it's not always entirely objective. Musicians in bands or ensembles often need to take the time to analyze songs and make agreements about what they consider to be the first beat, how to count out the song, where the pauses are, and if they, as a group, want to add pauses or change how long they hold certain notes. Sometimes musicians like to put their own spin on what they play, and although they may understand the timing of a song as written, they also might choose to play around with it a bit. This is part of what's called *arranging* a song. Either way, whether they're sticking with the song as written or modifying it, they need to understand and agree on how to count out the beats in their song so that they can play or sing it consistently and be in sync with their fellow musicians.

Counting Out the Beats in a Song

I love working with "Row, Row, Row Your Boat" because in one way its rhythm is very clear and easy to talk about, but in another way it's a bit trickier. So it offers the opportunity to describe a few concepts at once.

"The pleasure we obtain from music comes from counting, but counting unconsciously. Music is nothing but unconscious arithmetic."
-Gottfried Wilhelm Leibniz

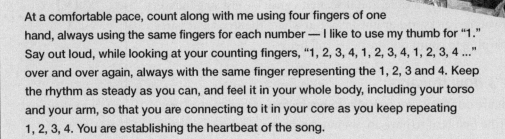

Note that when we studied this song in Chapter 17, we were working with its tonal aspects — the notes in the melody — and the numbers written above the words referred to the notes in the scale. Here, we are working with the song's rhythmic aspects and the numbers above the words will refer to the number of the beats.

**Exercise 19.1:
Counting Out the Main Beats
in Row, Row, Row Your Boat
Track 39 ◀)), Video 13 ▶**

At a comfortable pace, count along with me using four fingers of one hand, always using the same fingers for each number — I like to use my thumb for "1." Say out loud, while looking at your counting fingers, "1, 2, 3, 4, 1, 2, 3, 4, 1, 2, 3, 4 ..." over and over again, always with the same finger representing the 1, 2, 3 and 4. Keep the rhythm as steady as you can, and feel it in your whole body, including your torso and your arm, so that you are connecting to it in your core as you keep repeating 1, 2, 3, 4. You are establishing the heartbeat of the song.

```
1 - 2 - 3 - 4 - 1 - 2 - 3 - 4
1 - 2 - 3 - 4 - 1 - 2 - 3 - 4
```

Keep this strong, solid rhythm going with your body and fingers (keeping an eye on your fingers, so you can see the rhythm as well as feel it) but now instead of counting the numbers, say, "bum, bum, bum, bum" in sets of four. Many songs you'll be singing early on will have phrases that fit into sets of four beats, usually with the strongest beat on the 1 of the set, like this:

BUM bum bum bum BUM bum bum bum
BUM bum bum bum BUM bum bum bum

The beats are all evenly spaced from each other, but the 1 beat is the loudest, and marks the beginning of each phrase.

When you feel like you've got it, stop counting on your fingers for a while and instead gently tap your chest on each "bum."

Next, return to counting with your fingers (still keeping the feeling of the rhythm in your whole body), while reading along with the words and numbers below. Then finally, start singing the words of the song while following along below, and notice how the timing of the words fits into the 4 beats of each line of the song:

1	2	3	4
Row	Row	Row	Your Boat

1	2	3	4
Gently	Down	the Stream	(pause)

Notice that some of the words fall between the main beats.

1	2	3	4
Merrily,	Merrily,	Merrily,	Merrily

1	2	3	4
Life	is But	a Dream	(pause)

Do you see how the pulse of the song is always the same? The 1, 2, 3, 4 are always the same distance apart, and though many of the words fall right on the beat, some of them fall in between those four steady beats. I will refer to those in-between beats as "microbeats." Before we talk about microbeats in the next section, do the previous exercise a few more times to be sure that you're confident, both physically and cognitively, about singing Row, Row, Row Your Boat while counting out the beats.

Before moving on, answer the following questions:

• Did you feel a sense of a fresh start at the beginning of each phrase — how even though the beat never pauses throughout the whole song, each new phrase begins on the "1" beat?

• Do you agree that if you were to emphasize any of the beats in this song, it would probably be most natural if they were the "1" beats of each phrase?

• Do you see how having a clear sense of where the first beat of each phrase in this song occurs makes it easier for people to sing together and understand where to come in (which is especially important if they're singing it as a round)?

• Do you see how even though I'm telling you this, it's optional? If you chose to, you could put the emphasis on a different beat — on the 2, 3 or 4.

• Do you get that, if a musician was singing this song but wanted to jazz it up, there are infinite ways that he could play with the rhythm, giving punch to whatever beats he wanted?

Whether we are singing a song, or listening to one, an important part of the magic — what draws us in — is the steady underlying beat. Although musicians often vary the emphasis of the beats, or subdivide the beats into microbeats and play around with how they emphasize them, they usually keep the basic pulse of a song steady. When they don't, the effect is usually dramatic, making it feel almost as if we're moving on to a new song.

Counting Out Microbeats in Groups of Threes

Now, let's check out another aspect of the rhythm of "Row, Row, Row Your Boat." This is a little subtle and could be considered extra information. Just skip ahead if you think it's too much for you right now, or if you know all this already!

Because the first word of each phrase in "Row, Row, Row Your Boat" starts right on the "1" beat, this song is easy to count out in 4s, as we've been doing here. Now notice that there is an interesting rocking feel to the song between these beats. It's a great song because it's about rowing a boat down a stream and instead of having a choppy feel, it has a kind of circular feel, like oars circling around through air and water, doesn't it? And why is that? It's because the microbeats — the subdivisions between the main beats that we've been counting out so far — come in sets of threes.

This becomes clear when we sing the words "merrily." It takes three evenly-spaced syllables to get from one of the main beats to the next, and each of those syllables happen on each of the three microbeats. You'll see what I mean when you do the next exercise.

Exercise 19.2: Count Out the Microbeats in Row, Row, Row Your Boat
Track 40 🔊))

Pick three fingers to count on. Along with me, count out the micro-beats on your fingers (and watch your fingers!). Spend enough time doing this to register how counting out threes feels different from counting out fours.

1 - 2 - 3 - **1** - 2 - 3 - **1** - 2 - 3 - **1** - 2 - 3
1 - 2 - 3 - **1** - 2 - 3 - **1** - 2 - 3 - **1** - 2 - 3

Next, (and this is to help you get out of your intellect and more into the whole-body *feeling* of the threes), try rocking your whole body, or stepping from side to side as we sing, **BUM** bum bum **BUM** bum bum **BUM** bum bum **BUM** bum bum

Now, along with me, say,

1 - 2 - 3 - **2** - 2 - 3 - **3** - 2 - 3 - **4** - 2 - 3

Notice that this time, instead of starting each set of three with the number one, we are naming each of the main beats with a 1, 2, 3, or 4. We are now syncing up with the main beats of the song that we were singing before, in the last exercise, and getting the feeling of how the microbeats fit into the bigger beats.

Finally, join me in singing the song and notice how the words fall on both the main beats and the microbeats.

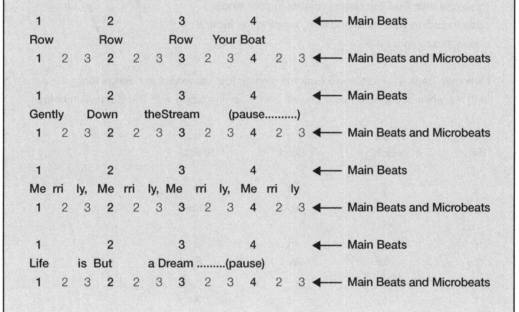

"Row, Row, Row Your Boat," offers you the opportunity to see how a song can be counted out in beat sets of threes and fours, with the larger beats grouped into fours and the microbeats grouped into threes. You now have a pretty good understanding of a song which has some interesting rhythmic aspects. Cool!

In the following song, we'll be counting out the main beat in sets of fours, just the way we did with Row, Row, Row Your boat, but instead of the microbeats occurring in sets of threes, here they will occur in sets of twos. These different beat and microbeat accents give a different feel to a song. See if you can get a sense of that as we move along.

Counting Out Microbeats in Groups of Twos

Exercise 19.3: Counting Out the Main Beats and the Microbeats in Bah, Bah, Black Sheep
Track 41 🔊))

Start by counting out fours on your fingers at a comfortable pace. Watch your fingers as you count and say out loud, "1, 2, 3, 4, 1, 2, 3, 4, 1, 2, 3, 4..." over and over again, always with the same finger representing the one, two, three and four. Feel the steady rhythm in your whole body including your torso and arm, keeping the motion connected to your core.

Now play Track 41. First, you'll hear me singing just the main beat. Sing along with me while counting on your fingers and following along with the Illustration below.

1		2		3	4
Bah		Bah		Black	Sheep

1		2		3	4
Have	you	a	ny	Wool	(Pause)

1		2		3	4
Yes		Sir		Yes	Sir

1		2		3	4
Three		Bags		Full	(Pause)

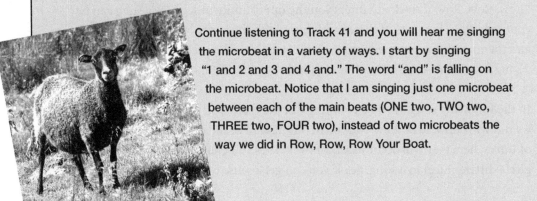

Photo by Malene Thyssen

Continue listening to Track 41 and you will hear me singing the microbeat in a variety of ways. I start by singing "1 and 2 and 3 and 4 and." The word "and" is falling on the microbeat. Notice that I am singing just one microbeat between each of the main beats (ONE two, TWO two, THREE two, FOUR two), instead of two microbeats the way we did in Row, Row, Row Your Boat.

Sing with Track 41 while following along with the illustration below. Notice which syllables of which words fall on the microbeats.

1		2		3		4		← Main Beats
Bah		Bah		Black		Sheep		
1	2	2	2	3	2	4	2	← Main Beats and Microbeats

1		2		3		4		← Main Beats
Have	you	a	ny	Wool		(Pause)		
1	2	2	2	3	2	4	2	← Main Beats and Microbeats

1		2		3		4		← Main Beats
Yes		Sir		Yes		Sir		
1	2	2	2	3	2	4	2	← Main Beats and Microbeats

1		2		3		4		← Main Beats
Three		Bags		Full		(Pause)		
1	2	2	2	3	2	4	2	← Main Beats and Microbeats

These are only two ways out of many to organize beats. There's a lot more to learn on this subject but here I just want you to have a basic sense of how identifying the rhythm of a song that you are working on can help you get your bearings and feel more confident.

Pickup Beats

In some songs (including both Row, Row, Row Your Boat and Bah, Bah, Black Sheep) the first strong beat occurs on the first word, so we start counting the beats from there. However, it doesn't always make musical sense to start counting on the very first word of a song. If you're singing along with an instrument, the first downbeat (on a guitar that might be the first strong strum) might not come on the first word.

An example of this is "This Land is Your Land." The first words of the song are "This land is," but we don't start counting the beats until the word "Your" because that's the first word that gets rhythmic emphasis, and because when you start there the whole song falls easily into place. The phrase "This Land Is" is what musicians call a *pickup*. Try singing along with Video 14 and see if you can feel what I'm talking about.

Exercise 19.4: Counting With a Pickup: "This Land Is Your Land"
Video 14 ▶

This Land is ◄——— That's the Pickup!

1		2		3		4	
Your		Land		(pause)	this	Land	is

1		2		3		4	
My		Land		(pause)	from	Cal	- i -

1		2		3		4	
for	-	nia		(pause)	to the	New	York

1		2		3		4	
Is	-	land	(pause)		from the Gulf	Stream	

and so on ...

This idea of a pickup might seem a little complicated, but over time and with experience, it becomes something you can feel. Once again, as is so often the case with music, there is no definitive right or wrong. Sometimes you just start counting from wherever is your best guess and see what happens as you move through the song. Try watching Video 14 again but this time start counting from the word "This" or the word "Land." Ultimately it's up to you where to start counting. Doing this might help you understand why we generally count this song starting on the word "Your" and why "This land is" is considered a pickup. You don't have to master this concept, but it is helpful to know what people mean when they refer to a pickup; it's good to know this concept if you are singing with other people.

If you're confused when trying to count out a song, it might be because the first words are actually a pickup, and come before the main beat.

To Sum It Up

How you think about the beat of a song, and how you figure out for yourself where to start singing different phrases, can be conceptualized in different ways. It depends on your goals and what makes it most interesting, or easiest, for you to grasp the concept in relation to any particular song.

For beginning singers, it's helpful to pick up cues from any instruments that are playing while you sing, and from any more experienced musicians around you. Having gone through the exercises in Chapters 18 and 19 will help you to have a feeling for the beat in your body (so very important) and to understand what those more experienced musicians are talking about.

You may hear musicians using terms like "time signature," and "2/4, 3/4, or 4/4" (or other mysterious sounding fractions), which are ways of referring to the concepts we've been discussing here. Don't let their jargon put you off. Ask them to explain what they mean, and remember that it all boils down to what we're talking about in these chapters: ways of tracking how songs move through time, predicting what parts of a song happen when, and getting to a point where you are feeling the beat in your body.

Photo by Jeff Delonge.
Mimlu Sen and Paban Das Baul, Bengali Baul musicians,
at the International Asian Film Festival in Vesoul, France.

Ice Breaker!

Ham it Up

Pick a song that moves you (don't worry about how well you're singing) and
take it all the way. Sing the song and tell its story. Make it so dramatic,
so over the top, that you can't imagine taking it any further.
Try pretending you're an opera singer or that you're in a musical, if that helps.
Use your whole body.

You might never choose to sing this way with other people,
but if you're embarrassed to do this even in front of yourself,
this ice breaker is the perfect opportunity for you to step out and take a chance.
Bring your self-expression out into the open! Play with it!

Do this both with and without a mirror.
And don't forget to be a great supportive, accepting audience for yourself!

Benefits
Allows you to fully
embody a song and
explore using your
voice to express
your emotions,
without worrying
about what other
people think.

Chapter 20
Create an Inspiring Warm-Up Routine

Whenever you start a singing session, it's ideal to begin with some kind of warm-up to get your body, your breath, and your voice stretched and ready. You want to remind your body of the connection between your diaphragmatic muscles and your voice, and allow your vocal apparatus to move around and remember specific intervals.

Simply put, it's better not to jump right into singing things that are difficult, but rather to work your way in gradually. It's great to warm up for 5-10 minutes but even just a minute or two makes a huge difference. Like everything else about singing, warm-ups work best when you do them with love and joy!

Warm-ups can be very informal. There are simple ways to warm up that work for any situation. Full-body warm-ups are great, but if that's not an option there are warm-ups that work just fine when you're in the car, in a hurry, or in a social situation where you don't want your warm-up to be conspicuous or a big deal.

There are lots of warm-up ideas in Appendix I. In Appendix II you will find a one-page "Handy Dandy Warm-Ups" tear-out that you can tack up on your wall or fridge.

The activities are separated into three groups:
• Full Body Warm-ups
• Voice and Breath Warm-ups
• Ear and Voice Tuning Warm-ups

Many of the activities are also found earlier in this book as part of the exercises, so they will be familiar. Choose a few to get started. Keep trying new ones over time and then, as you discover which ones you like best, mix and match them spontaneously to develop your own warm-up routine or a variety of routines for various settings.

Go to Appendix I for a big fat list of activities to use in your warm-ups!

"Sing before the spirits and dance with the earth deities And you will be able to compose your own tune. Then you and I, united, will clap hands joyously, Singing 'tum-tiddly-um tum-tiddly-um-tum."
– Hongzhi Zhengjue

"All the sounds of the earth are like music."
– Oscar Hammerstein

Photo by Bill Loewy, 1993. Kongar-ool Ondar, Tuvan throat singer.

Chapter 21:
Repetition, Muscle Memory, And Practicing

Repetition

Ever noticed how toddlers ask to have the same book read to them over and over? When you were a kid in school did you have to drill the multiplication tables or practice your vocabulary words by saying the definitions over and over until they were imprinted in your mind? As an adult, think about the things you have to do a LOT. Driving the same route, paying the bills, cooking dinner, doing the dishes, or the skills you need for your job or career. Do you notice that as you repeat actions you get better at them and that they come more easily (okay — maybe not so with paying the bills ...)? Even the best professional musicians have to practice before they go out there and do their stuff. For hours and hours and hours! They practice the same pieces and repeat the same licks over and over before they are prepared to perform them. It's through repetition that we develop the pathways in our brain and the memory in our muscles to do something so well that it looks (and sometimes truly becomes) easy.

Muscle Memory

An interesting example that applies to many people is typing on a keyboard. There was a time before you could type, when the physical action of finding each letter was difficult. The expression for that is (or was, when I was growing up) "hunt and peck." Your fingers didn't know where to go. You had to think about it. You had to look at the keys. But the more you did it the faster and more fluent you became, until you found that you were able to type fairly accurately without even looking. You developed muscle memory. If this example doesn't apply to you, I'm sure there is another skill you've mastered to which the idea of practicing and developing muscle memory can be applied.

We all have places in our lives where muscle memory kicks in. Let's go back to the "either you have it or you don't" myth about singing. Singers practice too — even those who seem to be born with the ability. Some singers may have had the aptitude to sing well practically from birth, and others may have had to put in a lot of conscious effort, but in either case, whether they're rigorously "practicing," singing for pure joy,

"If music be the food of love, play on."
– William Shakespeare

or working to master a particular song, they are learning through repetition just the way we all learn everything! Isn't this liberating? This means that when you are struggling to get the notes right in Row, Row, Row Your Boat, it doesn't mean you're hopeless. It means you're on the right track and doing what it takes to master an aspect of this new skill.

One important reason why singers practice scales is because it helps to stimulate and strengthen their muscle memory. The ability to adjust quickly from "1" note to another, whether up a scale or in a song, improves the more you do it; the muscles in your larynx learn how to move to create the pitch you want, the same way that your fingers learn how to find the letters on the keyboard.

If singing in tune is hard for you now, it will become easier. You may need to do a lot of repetition before muscle memory kicks in. If you are patient with yourself and repeat, repeat, repeat, you will get there.

Practicing – Keep it Fun!

Every person has their own approach to practicing. Some people like to create concrete goals and habits; others practice on the fly. To create a practice that works for you, let's start by discussing the concept of practice in general.

I like to think about practice as both a noun and a verb. I practice, and I have a practice. My practice is a gift to myself that nurtures and ultimately helps me thrive because it feeds my soul. Even if I only have a few minutes to dip in, it's worth it because it puts me in touch with the music, the intent, and the state of mind that my practice is all about. So in my world, every single effort I make to practice is worth it and valuable.

This includes singing in the car or in the shower; it includes grabbing my guitar for three minutes to sing a quick song; it includes teaching a singing lesson or practicing for a children's class. It actually includes the time I spend teaching those classes. It even includes thinking about music or listening to music on the radio. Of course it includes the times that I sit down for an hour or two and focus on the skills or songs that I want to learn at any given time; or the times that I get together with other people to practice for a performance. If I had a rigid definition of "practice" I wouldn't be able to succeed because I don't generally have big chunks of time to devote regularly to practicing. For me, practicing is a fluid thing that flows in and around the other important things in my life.

As I mentioned earlier in the book, one of my music teachers told me, "everything counts." As an example she told me that during a period in her life when she was having trouble making time for herself to practice playing the guitar, she put her guitar on its stand and placed it right in one of the doorways in her house. She couldn't go through that door without picking up the guitar and moving it! And as long as she had it in her hands anyway, she might as well spend a couple of minutes playing it. This is how she made sure she had some practice time each day with her guitar. Brilliant!

That said, I do also create longer, more focused practice sessions. Below is a list of elements I tend to include. Each element doesn't show up every time, but over the course of a week or a month I'm likely to get to all of the following activities or techniques.

Photo by Derek Bridges.
Walter Payton singing with his band, Gumbo Filé.

Elements You Might Include In Your Practice

- Breathing/stretching/vocal toning
    (any nice warm-up for your body and voice)
- S-s-s-s-s-sssssss's to remind your body to engage
    the diaphragmatic muscles
- Some intuitive quiet sound/voice explorations
- Some loud big-energy sounds (possibly some Heys)
- Pitch-matching practice using a drone as a home base,
  or singing or parts of the scale
- Singing a familiar, comfortable song
- Studying and singing a new, more challenging song
- Moving around while singing
- Singing with accompaniment
  (even just tapping out the beat is a form of accompaniment)
- Singing along to recorded music
- Singing with other people

Go to Appendix I for a list of warm-ups to choose from.

I often approach my practice sessions as if I were building a club sandwich; the easier stuff is the bread and the harder stuff is the contents of the sandwich. I start and finish with easy stuff and put the harder stuff that requires more focused concentration into the middle. But like that piece of bread in the middle of a club sandwich, I like to pop a little something that's easy and satisfying into the middle, to keep me feeling connected and happy. So, it's like this: easy, harder, easy, harder, easy.

A look at a random Nancy practice session (about a half hour to 45 minutes long):

Something Easy to Start:

• Physical warm-up with big breathing (maybe some stretches, Sssss's and some big Hey sounds).

• Loose singing explorations possibly accompanied by simple instrument playing (a drum, a chord on the piano, a chord or two on my guitar).

• Singing a song I know and love.

The More Challenging Part:

• Working on a new song — separating out the parts that are difficult into small bites and repeating them to build music memory. This might mean focusing on how the rhythm works in the song, going over the melody and repeating the intervals that I find difficult, or repeating the words over and over to memorize them.

Then, if I start to get frustrated or feel that I need a break ...

Another Easy Part:

• Something easy and gratifying — maybe a little improvising with a drone or singing a song I've been singing for years but putting a ton of expression into it.

A Little More Hard Stuff:

• Going back to the tricky new song I was just working on, or something else that's challenging.

Something Fun and Easy to Finish Up With:

• Singing a different song that comes easily, or just doing some fun improvising.

Club Sandwich
Practice Session

It's Important to Have Fun All Along the Way!

I feel strongly that practice should be rewarding and fun. This is especially true for older people who, for better or worse, have gotten by their whole lives without much singing. You're a busy person with a lot of other, perhaps easier, things to do. Maybe singing is important, but is it important enough to fit into your life if it's grueling drudgery, full of boring repetition? I think probably not! This is why it's so important to invite the muse — to stay in touch with the beauty and intuition that we explored in the first part of this book. You need to alternate WORK with PLAY when you practice, until they become one. I like that so much, I'm going to repeat it in great big letters.

Alternate WORK with PLAY until they become one.

So, use the following sample practice session to give you an idea of how you might structure a practice session of your own.

Something Easy to Start:
• Loosen up by humming, sirening, or making some crazy sounds.
• Engage your body with a stretching and breathing warm-up.

The More Challenging Part:
• Work on scale patterns using a piano or a recording, or with a friend.
• Spend a few minutes working on a song. It's okay to get a little bit frustrated but not TOO frustrated; if you're too frustrated …

Another Easy Part:
• Get up and move around and do something relaxing for a minute or two.
  Put on a drone and improvise to it — sing something expressive.
  Or put on a favorite song and dance and sing along with it. Stretch. Breathe.
  Meanwhile the activity that was getting frustrating may have jelled somewhat
  in your subconscious so when you return to it again it's easier.

A Little More Hard Stuff:
• Now maybe it's time to go back to the scale pattern or the challenging song.
  See if a little audiating helps.

Something Fun and Easy to Finish Up With:
• Do whatever appeals to you now. Remember why you want to learn to sing —
  remember that singing can touch your soul. Maybe you want to go deeper, try out
  a new song, get a tapping rhythm going on a drum or a table and improvise a song
  with that rhythm as your accompaniment. Maybe you want to sing loud or
  dramatically. Follow your impulses. Stay in touch with how you're feeling. End
  your practice session with something that gives you a sense of satisfaction.

There is another version of this list for you to tear out and use as a handy reference on page 227, Appendix II.

A practice session can last hours or take just a few minutes. Do this on your own terms, in whatever way suits you best at any given time. Let every practice session be as musical, playful, beautiful, expressive, and fun as it can be!

Photo by Alexandre Delbos. Street musicians in Madrid.

Chapter 22
Building Your Repertoire

Here's how this chapter works. I have created a list of songs that I like and that I think are good choices for beginners. With some of the songs, you'll find tips and hints to guide you through the learning process. Once you've tried using the tips with these songs you'll be able to apply these ideas to the other songs on the list, as well as to any other songs that interest you. Many of these songs might be familiar. Most are easy to find, both as audio tracks and videos online and written out in musical notation. Choose a song you like, find a version to listen to, and learn it by using a combination of the following (by now familiar) methods:

- Listen to it over and over. Sing along with it loosely, not worrying about right or wrong.

- Sing along with it analytically, noticing the shape of the song. Where are the highest notes? The lowest notes? Do several chunks of the song have the same melody? Where are the pauses? What's the most intuitive way to count out the beats? Refer to Chapters 17-19 for support.

- Find the "1" note and figure out how the other notes compare to it. Often the *last* note of a song will be the 1. ***Unless noted, all the songs referred to in this chapter end on the 1 of the scale that they are sung in.***

- Sing it with expression and be real, connecting to the genuine feeling that the words and melody of the song evoke in you.

- Check in to be sure that you're comfortable, and not tensing up your shoulders or throat.

- Be sure to support your voice by powering it with your diaphragm (do the S-s-s-s-s exercise to refresh your memory).

Note that when I make reference to specific words in these songs, I am taking them from the first verse only. Once you've understood what's happening in the first verse you can go on to work out for yourself the other verses in each song.

The more you do it, the easier it gets. It's a way of thinking. It's a language. Each time you learn a new song, print out the words and write your tips and hints about that song on your songsheet. Keep all your songsheets together in a folder or binder so they are handy for practicing with, and as a reference if singing opportunities arise with friends.

"Every child is an artist. The problem is how to remain an artist once we grow up."
– Pablo Picasso

"Row, Row, Row Your Boat"
Melody: Starts on the 1, first three notes are the same, the lowest note in the whole song is the 1, the highest note is the 8 (the same note as the 1 but an octave higher) and occurs on the 3 syllables of the first "me-rri-ly." Each syllable of each of the four merrilys are all on the same note; the first "merrily" is the highest and the following ones move steadily lower; in the last line, "life is but a dream" is sung one note per syllable, moving down the scale like this: 5-4-3-2-1.

Rhythm: There are four beats in each phrase, but the microbeat occurs in sets of three (as in "me-rri-ly").

"This Land is Your Land"
Note: This song has a lot of words; start by just working on the first verse!

Melody: The melody starts on the 1 note. The first line, "This land is your land," goes 1-2-3-4-4. The melody dips down below the 1 on the last line, with the very lowest note happening on the words, "made for."

Rhythm: Works best when you start counting the beats on the word "your," so that "This land is ..." at the very beginning is a pickup. After that, count out the main beats in sets of four. All throughout the song, the phrases start before the first main beat. Try it and you'll see what I mean.

"You Are My Sunshine"
Note: This song is much simpler to sing than it is to talk about!

Melody: When learning the melody it helps to think of each verse as having four lines:

Line 1: You are my sunshine, my only sunshine
Line 2: You make me happy, when skies are grey
Line 3: You'll never know dear, how much I love you
Line 4: Please don't take my sunshine away

The melody starts on the 5 below the 1 (with the word "You"). So, if you're singing it in C, the starting note is the G from the octave below (that's also the lowest note in the whole song). Lines one, three and four all end on the 1 note. Lines two and three have exactly the same melody except for the very end (the word *you* in line three). So once you've learned line two, you've pretty much learned line three. The highest notes in the song are in the middle of the phrases on lines 2 and 3 ("py - when" and "dear - how").

Rhythm: Count out the beats in fours. The first words, "You are my," are a pickup; start counting out the song on the word "sunshine."

"The Happy Birthday Song"

Note: Because this song is so commonly sung, people think of it as an easy song — but it's not that easy. It hops around in unusual ways and has a wide range (a pretty big distance from the lowest note to the highest note). Thinking it should be easy but still having a hard time with it can be the cause of much singing discouragement, as in the sentiment, "I'm such a lousy singer that I can't even sing the Happy Birthday Song!" So take it easy on yourself, and try out these tips.

Melody: Starts on the 5 below the 1; that's also the lowest note in the song. People tend to start this song too high, not anticipating how high that will place the highest note, and that it might be hard to reach. So, if you're in charge, start nice and low.

Each line of this song is a little higher on average than the line before it, with the very highest note being on the syllable "Birth" in line 3. That note is the high 5. Notice how you're getting to that highest note: you're jumping to it from the low 5. That's a whole octave! That's kind of tricky, but after that it's just a steady stepping down to the last word of that third line. Here are the notes of the melody of the Happy Birthday song:

low 5 low 5   low 6   low 5   1   low 7
Happy Birthday to You,

low 5 low 5   low 6   low 5   2   1
Happy Birthday to You,

low 5 low 5   5   3   1   low 7 low 6
Happy Birthday Dear Calvin,

4   4   3   1   2   1
Happy Birthday to You

Rhythm: This song is in 3/4 rhythm, meaning that the beats occur in sets of 3 instead of sets of 4. Actually, I urge you to only think about this if you're truly interested; otherwise just go with the flow and feel the rhythm in your body and don't worry about analyzing it. This is one of those times when thinking too much can mess you up. For those of you who are curious, however, here is how the rhythm works in the Happy Birthday song ... The first "Happy" is a pickup, so you don't start counting until the word "Birthday"

(pickup)
Happy   *bum* *bum*   *bum* *bum*
1 | | 2 | |
Birthday   to   You,   Happy
3 | | 4 | |
Birthday   to   You,   Happy
5 | | 6 | |
Birthday dear Calvin,   Happy
7 | | 8 | |
Birthday   to   You........

Count out 1-bum-bum, 2-bum-bum, and so on, with the larger emphasis on the number and lighter emphasis on the bum-bum. This will help you to embody the feeling of singing in threes (or 3/4 time).

AND, people play like crazy with the rhythm of this song, stretching out some lines for fun — so really, just go with the flow as best you can and try to enjoy whatever happens!

Undoubtedly, you will have the opportunity to sing the Happy Birthday song again, and my biggest piece of advice is to relax and enjoy it. On the one hand it's an opportunity to try out some of your new concepts and skills, and on the other hand it will go by in a flash and soon you will get to eat cake. Mostly, don't fall into the trap of thinking that how well you can sing this song is an indication of whether or not you have potential as a singer. That just isn't true, and doing that takes all the fun out of it!

"Michael Row Your Boat Ashore," Traditional African American Spiritual
Melody: The first three syllables, "Mi - chael - row" are on the notes 1-3-5. You know how to sing that — you've been practicing that combination of notes! This song has a small range, even though it may not sound that way. The melody never dips below the 1 and the highest it ever goes is to the 6 — that happens in the first line on the first syllable of the word "ashore" and on the "lu" syllable of the word "hallelujah."

Rhythm: This is in 4/4 time: count out the beats in groups of four. There's no pickup, just start counting on "Michael."

"Hey Jude," by Lennon-McCartney (original version as performed by the Beatles)
Note: You won't find the 1 note by listening for the last note in this song (they do some crazy riffing there at the end). Listen instead for the last note of the first verse — that's the 1.

Melody: Let's start by talking about the first verse: The first two notes ("Hey, Jude") are 5-3. The word "song" (... take a sad "song") is an octave up from the 1. The highest note in the verse (and the whole song, actually) is "let" (... remember to "let"). The lowest note occurs on the first syllable of the word "better" in the last line. It's just a half step lower than the 1. That's actually the lowest note of the whole song as well.

Now let's take a look at the shape of the whole song.

• The first two verses have the same tune.

• Then there's a bridge, which has a different tune.

• Verse three has the same tune as the earlier verses.

• Then there's another bridge with basically the same tune as the first bridge but with some variation where it goes higher.

• The final verse has basically the same tune (and words) as the first verse with the exception of some wiggly extras on the word "Jude." The "nah-na-na-nas" at the end are fun to sing along with. This exercises your listening skills, doesn't it?

Rhythm: Count out the beats in fours. Start counting on the word "Jude."

"Bohemian Rhapsody," by Freddie Mercury / Queen
Melody & Rhythm: Don't worry about anything — just sing it and sing loud!

Fairly Simple Songs You Might Enjoy Learning:

"Blue Moon," *Richard Rodgers and Lorenz Hart*

"Jingle Bells," *James Lord Pierpont (who knew?!)*

"Riding on the City of New Orleans," *Steve Goodman (made famous by Arlo Guthrie)*

"Wagon Wheel," *Bob Dylan, and Ketch Secor of Old Crow Medicine Show*

"Yellow Submarine," *Lennon-McCartney /The Beatles*

"I'm Yours," *Jason Mraz (**doesn't end on the "1," or root note**)*

"Rivers of Babylon," *Boney M*

"Imagine," *John Lennon*

"Mad World," *Gary Jules / Tears For Fears*

"No Woman No Cry," *Bob Marley and the Wailers (there's a beautiful story about why this song is credited to Vincent Ford — go check it out!)*

"Oh, What a Beautiful Morning," *Rodgers and Hammerstein, from Oklahoma!*

"May The Circle Be Unbroken," *Ada R. Habershon & Charles H. Gabriel*

"Take Me Home, Country Roads," *John Denver*

"Tumbalaika," *Traditional Russian Jewish folk song in Yiddish*

"Angel Band," *Jefferson Hascall & J. W. Dadmun*

"500 Miles," *Hedy West*
   (sometimes also credited to Curly Williams, and/or John Phillips as co-writers)

"I'll Fly Away," *Albert E. Brumley*

"Bring Me Little Water Silvie," *Leadbelly*

"Sweet Caroline," *Neil Diamond (**trails off and doesn't end on the "1"**)*

"You Can Close Your Eyes," *James Taylor (**doesn't end on the "1"**)*

"Sometimes I Feel Like a Motherless Child," *Traditional*

"Summertime," *Music by George Gershwin, Lyrics by DuBose Heyward*

"Feliz Navidad," *Jose Feliciano*

Harder But Super Fun Songs to Sing Along With:

"Bohemian Rhapsody," *Freddie Mercury / Queen*

"We Will Rock You," *Brian May / Queen*
   *(**ends on the root note, but an octave up on the "8"**)*

"Yesterday," *Paul McCartney / The Beatles (**doesn't end on the "1"**)*

"If I Were a Rich Man," *Sheldon Harnick and Jerry Bock / Fiddler on the Roof*
   *(**ends on the root note, but an octave up on the "8"**)*

"Space Oddity," *David Bowie*

"Secret Agent Man," *P. F. Sloan and Steve Barri*

"Sunny Afternoon," *Ray Davies / The Kinks (**another one that ends on the "8"**)*

"Piano Man," *Billy Joel*

"Hey Jude," *Lennon-McCartney / The Beatles*
   *(**doesn't end on the "1" but you can find it at the end of the first verse**)*

Fun Songs to Sing With the Kids in Your Life:

"Eensy Weensy Spider," *Traditional*

"Six Little Ducklings," *Traditional*

"Mr. Golden Sun," *Traditional*

"Open Shut Them," *Traditional*

"Mr. Golden Sun," *Raffi*

"Baby Baluga," *Raffi*

"The Wheels on the Bus," *Lydia Ulsaker*

"If You're Happy and You Know It," *Lyrics refined by Alfred B. Smith*

"You Are My Sunshine," *Author Unknown*

"Down in the Valley, Two by Two," *Traditional southern play-party song*

**Photo by Christian Bertrand | Dreamstime.com.
The singers of Hinds (band also known as Deers)
performs at Heliogabal Club in Barcelona, Spain.**

Chapter 23
Moving Into the Rest of Your Life As a Singer

This is about integrating what you have learned and experienced into the rest of your life so that you actually continue to use it. Entry into the world of singing can change you — in fact, that's what it's all about, isn't it?

When you've opened the door for yourself to something as visceral, personal, and downright profound as singing, you've taught yourself something about what you're capable of, besides just the skills of learning to sing. Perhaps one of these applies to you:

- You're braver than you thought you were.
- You're more expressive than you thought you were.
- You're able to learn in ways you didn't know you could.
- You're able to hear in ways you didn't think you could.
- You are able to enjoy and perhaps appreciate the sound of your own voice.
- You can now speak the language of music with other people.
- You had the chutzpah to tell the nay-sayers whatever needed to be said.
- You have found a new wonderful and cool way to enjoy yourself!

Perhaps you've even started singing more comfortably at parties, in church, or wherever singing occurs in your world. Maybe you've gone to a karaoke night or joined a chorus. Maybe you're singing lullabies to your kids or grandchildren, or inventing songs of your own.

Whatever changes have happened in your life in relationship to singing are precious. We don't want to let them become buried in the busyness and habits of everyday life. You worked hard for these changes and now is the time to think about how to keep them alive and vibrant.

How do you keep growing as a singer? That's what this final chapter is about.

"Sing your own song,
Dance your own dance,
Dream your own dream,
Stake your own chance."
— Evette Carter

Creating Your Own Songbook

As part your new identity as a singer, I think it's important for you to create your own personal songbook. It's good for your mindset as a singer (even a "beginning singer," as opposed to a "non-singer"), and it's very important from a practical standpoint to have easy access to your tools. These, for the most part, are your warm-ups, favorite exercises, and songs, both as recordings and on paper. (I prefer paper to digital methods, but the times they are a'changing.) Apply the ideas below to whatever method works best for you.

My recommendation is to use a 3-ring binder divided into at least three sections including Warm-Ups & Practice, Tips and Reminders, and Songs.

Photo by © Viacheslav Dyachkov | Dreamstime.com. Nadezhda Babkina, prominent folk singer of Russian national songs.

What you'll need for your songbook "tool-kit":

• 3-ring binder with dividers and paper

• 3-ring hole punch

• A pen or pencil
  (So you can mark up the pages with your notes, jot down websites that friends suggest you check out, write down suggestions you're given, etc.)

• Wite-Out (trust me)

• Access to a printer or copier
  (For printing out pages from this book, from the website, words to songs that you want to copy from books, download from a computer or songsheets that you are given by friends, etc.)

Your *Warm-Ups & Practice* pages might include a copy of the "Handy-Dandy Warm-Up Tear-Out Sheet" on page 223, or copies of more detailed descriptions of any of your favorite exercises from this book or elsewhere. "Practice Session Ideas Tear-Out Sheet," on page 225, is another list that you might want to put into your book. Copy them onto an 8½ x 11 sheet of paper and punch holes in them with a 3-ring hole punch so you can pop them right into your binder. Add new ideas as you come across them or develop them yourself.

The Tips and Reminders section would include any ideas from this book (or elsewhere) that you found particularly helpful. Continue to be on the lookout for ideas to add to this section of your book!

In the Songs section, I think it's a great idea to put your songsheets (the pages with the lyrics to your songs) into alphabetical order and, if you find that your collection is growing sizable, to create a table of contents as well. I leave a big margin in my table of contents pages so that when I add a new song to the binder I have space to jot down the song name there. Then when I have time I can tidy up the table of contents in the computer, adding in the new titles and putting them into alphabetical order. That way I can see all the songs I have at a glance.

One great advantage of having this binder is that it makes it easy to communicate with other people about singing together. Especially if you are nervous it is great to have a list of songs that you like or have mastered, or even just know part of, to show other people. You can open to the table of contents or hand them the book and say, "Do you know any of these?" and without having to do much else, you've got the ball rolling.

Songsheets can contain more resources than just lyrics. Other elements that might also be on your songsheets are guitar chords (great if you or any of your friends happen to play the guitar), or musical notation (great if you or any of your friends read music and need a reminder of how the tune goes, or if anyone wants to do a piano accompaniment).

Your songsheets are also a great place to jot down any tips or reminders you have made for yourself about how the song works. Scribble down the kinds of notes that will prompt you enough so that you can find the groove of the song. For example "Starts on the 5 below the 1" can help you get going on the song, "You Are My Sunshine," and a little scribble that says, "Starts: 1-2-3-4-4" might be enough to propel you into the song, "This Land is Your Land." I do this kind of thing all the time.

Your songbook becomes a real treasure. I actually made 2 copies of mine; one to carry around with me when I go to parties or events and another as backup in case anything should happen to the one I travel with. Your songbook is as rich and useful as you make it. Draw in it or decorate it if you want. Love it up, because it is your self-made singing companion. Just opening up your songbook can be an inspiration and put you into a singing mood.

And it is a work in progress. Remember to add to it whenever you learn a new song and it will give you the kind of satisfaction you get from tending a healthy plant. Watch it grow with you as you grow as a singer.

Singing with Other People

Don't wait until you're a great singer to sing with other people. You don't need to be so skilled that you could lead the song you're singing, that you could perform it, or even that you could sing it alone without anyone to lean on. It's fine to just lay back and be part of the chorus or even to just hum. You don't need to sing loud, or even to know a whole song. Just sing the parts you feel comfortable with. The more often you put your voice out there and join in with other voices, the faster you'll learn.

Singing with other people doesn't need to be high stress. It's a mistake to think of it as a culmination of your singing efforts; instead think of every occasion to sing with other people as an opportunity to practice. Each time will be different and some times will be more fun than others. When it's less fun, don't succumb to old feelings of shame, but rather turn towards curiosity and see what you can learn.

Show yourself some appreciation for your courage. Acknowledge that even though the people around you might not know it, the fact that you're singing with them is an accomplishment!

Bring a Resilient Attitude to Deal with a Worst Case Scenario

If you have a rough singing history, you may find that your old traumas return to some extent when you first start taking your new singing skills out on the road. You might find yourself singing off-key, getting some funny looks from people, or even just not getting the positive feedback you were hoping for. Even the vacuum created by people saying nothing can make you feel criticized. This is not a signal to give up!

Even if the situation is seemingly casual or relaxed, it may trigger some of your old reactions. You might find yourself shaking, thinking negative thoughts, feeling self-conscious or embarrassed, or experiencing any number of the symptoms of fear.

Although you know that your skills have been improving, you may still be very sensitive about how people respond to you when you sing. Knowing that this is normal and that it will pass is comforting. Use your techniques from Chapters 8 and 9. Work with yourself to let embarrassment be just embarrassment — remind yourself that you do not have to move into the realm of shame. Shame says, "You are not worthy. You are alone." Embarrassment says, "This is awkward but it will pass. Everyone feels this way sometimes." You can expect to feel a little embarrassment now and then, and you can handle it. Let it go as fast as you can and line up your next opportunity speedy-quick so you don't get stuck. You'll start to experience less and less embarrassment and begin having more and more fun.

Choose Opportunities That Suit You

How do know what opportunities are right for you? You might be tempted to decline opportunities that arise feeling that you're not ready, so think now about setting intentions so that you won't succumb to panic and decline automatically. Don't let "no" be your default response.

Imagine that a friend of yours invites you to a Karaoke party. Do you want to go? If so, do you want to sing, or just watch? Standing up and singing in front of a group of people might be more than you want to do at this point. This opportunity, cool as it might sound, might not be in sync with where you are right now. If it's too much of a trigger of stage fright for you, saying no might be a good choice. While you're not allowing no to be your default, you don't have to say yes to everything. Try not to be on automatic pilot with your answers. Check in with yourself; question your first impulse and think it through. If you've thought about it and decided that you're not ready and your answer is no, that's perfectly fine.

On the other hand, perhaps you know that the crowd you'd be with is going is very supportive and that this opportunity, though a stretch, might be a good one. Go with your gut. Trust yourself, but make sure that part of the deal is that if you don't like what happens, you move right on and try something else.

Here's another scenario: You're at a Christmas party and people start singing carols. Your first impulse is to feel kind of left out as you have in the past. Then you think, "This is an opportunity!" You try humming along, but there's only one song you know well enough to really sing along with and they're not singing it. You're not confident enough yet to lead this song but you realize that if you ask the group someone there will probably know it. So you go ahead and ask, and pretty soon they're singing that song and you're singing too, and it's really fun and satisfying. Good job!

Another scenario: You're planning your son's birthday party and you know that everyone will expect the Happy Birthday Song at cake time. Usually you dread this but now you have a plan. You've been practicing and you know that you like to sing it pretty low, so instead of waiting for someone else to start it, you're going to take charge by getting the song started. You'll sing the first two syllables of the song (Hap-py...) loud and slow, so that everyone joins in at *your* pitch. You know that momentum will take over from there so you can just relax and let the rest of the song happen. You're proud that you actually got the song going — that was a big step for you. And you're happy that you could easily sing along because it was pitched in a comfortable key for you. Success!

Think about what opportunities are coming up and which ones you can create for yourself. What feels like too much? What sounds like fun? Does singing a song to your grandchild sound scarier or less scary than singing in a chorus? Start with what seems most comfortable and move gradually into opportunities that are more challenging. If you were to pick three activities, which would you prefer to come first, second and third? Jot down a few ideas and then turn on your radar for what comes your way.

Finding People to Sing With

If you look around, you might find some of these opportunities, or similar ones, in your community:

- Parties where people like to sing
- Singing around a campfire
- Weekly or monthly casual sing-along groups
- Choruses that are beginner-friendly
- Singing songs or chanting in your place of worship
- Friendly groups of people who like to jam in the living room
- Kirtan (Yogic chanting done in groups)
- Singing kids songs with your children or grandchildren
- Singing lullabies to help these children get to sleep
- Saying the "Ohm" at the end of a yoga class
- Elementary or preschool settings where there is singing in the classroom
- Senior Centers with music programming
- Singing classes or workshops with a great teacher and a supportive group of students
- Community theater musicals — start with a part in the chorus and go from there
- Singing with friends to the radio or device in the car

If opportunities to sing are not easily apparent, start asking around. Be specific about your skill level to increase the likelihood that the suggestions will work for you. "Classes for beginners," "community choruses that include inexperienced singers," and "informal groups where people play and sing just for fun," are a few phrases that might capture what you're looking for.

Touchstones for Creating Positive Experiences: Listening, Assessing and Blending

Sometimes you will be singing because it's been a planned activity. You may have practiced a few songs and want to try them out with a friend or in a group. You might have your songsheets with you, all marked up with your tips and reminders.

Other times, you may find yourself in a singing situation that you hadn't planned and you would like to join in.

Either way, there are many musical and social cues to listen for when you are singing with a group. You can't tune in to them all at once, all the time. But reading the following list will help you understand some of the touchstones that people often use to help themselves feel comfortable and sing better in a group setting.

TOUCHSTONES: Your Bag of Tricks for Social Singing Situations

• *Listen to the conversation and tone of the room. Make a quick assessment of where this group is on the "serious to laid back" spectrum.*

If the setting seems to be one where people are likely to be perfectionistic or critical, or if the vibe is very performance oriented, check in with yourself about whether it's probable that this will be a positive experience. Maybe the time is right for stepping up and taking a chance; on the other hand, remember that the optimal experiences for you at this stage will be supportive ones. A relaxed atmosphere where people are singing together as a fun community activity is more likely to offer friendly support.

• *Listen A LOT to find your place in the song.*

Use your listening skills (Chapter 11) to help you find and keep your place in the song. You want to sing quietly enough so that you can hear what's going on around you. You want to listen as much as possible so that when you sing you can compare and contrast and modify your singing as you go along.

• *Listen for, and sing along with, the "1."*

Notice where the verses of the song end and hum along with that note. This will help you locate the root note (what we've been calling the "1") with your own voice and will make you much more grounded in the whole song. It might even help you to understand the structure of the song and be better able to visualize its ups and downs.

• *Listen so that you can blend.*

This is a judgement call. Are you feeling relaxed and in a setting where it's not a big deal if you make a mistake? Are you feeling solid and resilient in the event that someone makes a comment? If you're feeling really confident — well, go for it! Sing out and don't worry about blending, go wild!

Photo by© Bondsza | Dreamstime.com. *African Choir Singers.*

On the other hand, you might want to blend.

Blending is what the singers in a chorus do so that together they create one unified sound. You blend by singing loud enough to hear yourself but quietly enough to still hear the other singers. I think of my voice as creating a net that lies just under the other voices and helps support them. I take a lot of cues from the other singers when I'm blending. I listen carefully to their pitch, their volume, and also to their vocal quality. Do they sound airy or constrained? Are they using vibrato (vibrato is a kind of a quivery sound like an opera singer might use) or are their voices keeping it simple? *To blend, I'm offering my voice into the mix as **more** of what's already there.* I'm listening and imitating and going with the flow. Most beginners are pretty happy to blend! Here's a little trick to help your blending go well ...

Gary Owens of Laugh-In, making a trademark announcement on the show from "Beautiful Downtown Burbank."

• *Do this silly thing ... it helps with blending.*
If you cup your fingers over your ear and aim the heel of your hand towards your mouth (like the announcer from the show, Laugh-In, on the left) you kind of shoot your voice right into your own ear. If you don't want to sing loud but you're having trouble hearing yourself this is a great little trick. Fool around with the exact placement of your fingers in relation to your ear, and your hand to your mouth for the best results. This works a little differently for each person. See Video 15. ▶

• *Keep your body engaged.*
Breathing, engaging the diaphragm, and feeling the beat in your body are all great ways to stay grounded and comfortable. Remember that you're doing this because you want to, for fun! If counting out beats on your fingers is easy and helpful — do it now! If tuning into the vibrations of sound helps you to stay on pitch — do it now! Staying engaged with your body helps keep you connected to the love!

• *Songs go by fast, like a moving train — listen for repetition.*
Hop on where you can, stay on as long as you can, and feel free to hop off when its lost you. Many songs have a chorus or a part that repeats. Listen for the parts that are easiest so that when they come around again you can hop back on!

• *Bring your song book or sheets along with you if you can.*
If you know you're heading out to a singing opportunity be sure to grab any support materials that you have, including your song book. If you use a car to get around you might want to keep a copy of your song book in the car so that it's always available when spontaneous singing moments arise.

Congratulations!

I hope your journey has been a wonderful one
and that it will continue to grow richer and more multifaceted
as you move deeper into your life as a person who sings.

Please stay in touch via my website and let me know how it goes,
and if you have any questions.

Happy Singing!
Love,

Nancy S.

Acknowledgments

I want to send a deep and heartfelt thanks to all the singing and music mentors I've known throughout my life, including Ethel Raim, Paul Brown, Bela Fleck, Val Mindel, Liza Constable and Julie Weber. Singing has always been the very best kind of therapy for me, so while you may have thought you were just giving music lessons, I know that you helped me grow as a whole person in the deepest and best ways possible. Every musical learning experience I've had has translated directly into a life learning experience and an emotional healing, so you all have been my treasured personal gurus. I am so grateful.

Thank you to Music Together® for giving me my first opportunity to discover how much I love being a songleader and music teacher. What an amazing program and incredible, supportive group of people you have put together!

To the Music for People community, founders David Darling and Bonnie Insull, all the amazing leaders and organizers, and to all my musical soulmates there, I owe thanks for bringing it all together, providing a path for my inner self and inner musician to step out and thrive in the outside world. From the first evening of my first workshop with you, it's felt like a miracle that something as organic and magical as music improvisation and facilitation could be taught. You opened up my heart and now music flies right out of it.

Endless thanks to my husband Forrest, and our kids Emily and Jacob, who believed that I could and should do this thing, even though this project was sometimes like an ocean liner plowing through our daily life, pushing aside other tasks and concerns in its wake (particularly vacuuming and cooking); thank you for understanding, picking up the slack, and for loving me so much! Thank you also for your great ideas and feedback along the way — you are such smart, thoughtful people and great to bounce ideas back and forth with. Boy, I just can't even express how lucky I feel that you guys are my family.

Thanks to the many friends and family who helped me over the five years it took to complete this project. Your perspective, thoughtful feedback, encouragement and enthusiasm were invaluable: in particular Ethan Salwen, Peter Salwen, Peggy Salwen, William Salwen, James Salwen, Joan Klagsbrun, Carla Turoff, Stacia Tolman,

Amy Benedict, Susan Hay, Kath McLaughlin, George Ponzini, Damien Licata, Joanne Lutz, Mark Lesses, and Caddy Gregory.

Thank you also to my music buddies, Judith Stone, J.B. Mack, Guy Soucy and Liza Constable. Onward and Upward!

Thank you so much to the following people for contributing your skills, expertise and time: Tom Bassarear, Zach Benton, Kat Wood, Siri Rosendahl, Emma Kipp, Jeanne Marie Eayrs, Helaine Iris, Sean Wiley, and Maddie Weinreich. Thank you to the photographers who gave me permission to use your beautiful photos.

Thank you to all of you who contributed financially to the IndieGoGo campaign, and especially to my aunt, Bernice Turoff — you have always believed in me! You all made this happen, and showd me that there was enthusiasm for this idea.

And to the FFF: Susan, Amy, Kristina, and Marcia — you are the fuel in my tank!

Finally, to all my students and workshop participants. It may sound cliché, but I can't think of a better way to say it; working with you has truly been an honor. Thank you so very much for sharing your voices with me and being so darn brave.

And Dad, "You'll always know your neighbor,
you'll always know your pal,
if you've ever navigated on the Erie Canal."
Fun singing with you!
I treasure those moments.

Appendices

Appendix I
Warm-Up Activities to Use in Your Practice Sessions
•
Appendix II
Handy-Dandy Warm-Up Tear-Out Sheet
•
Appendix III
Sample Practice Session Tear-Out Sheet
•
Appendix IV
Resources: Books, CDs, Videos, Websites & Organizations

U.S. Navy Photo by Gillian Brigham, Dar es Salaam, Tanzania, 2007.
U.S. Navy Europe-Africa Band musicians sing a popular African song
with children at Yatima Group Orphanage.

Photo by B. R. Ramana Reddi, 2013. Hindu Harikatha singers sing devotional songs at Sankranti Festival in South India.

Appendix I
Warm-Ups

These warm-ups are divided into three sections:

Full Body Warm-Ups
Voice and Breath Warm-Ups
Ear and Voice Tuning Warm-Ups

Ideally your warm-up will include at least one activity
from each group.

Since many of the warm-ups in this chapter can also be found in other parts
of this book, some of the instructions here will be fairly brief.
Refer to the accompanying page numbers for more details on these activities.

Full Body Warm-Ups

Yoga Stretch with Breath and Sound
From Chapter 10, page 105. Video #3

Standing, or sitting towards the front edge of a chair, imagine a string pulling
you up from the back of the top of your head. Let your ribs be gently lifted,
and be sure that your shoulders, neck, jaw and face are as relaxed as possible.

Breath in as you reach up over your head with you arms and hands.
Reach up to the sky for a moment and when you are full of breath, let out a nice
loud sigh as you stretch your arms and hands up, out and then slowly back down
to your sides. Do it a few times until you feel nice and stretched out.
Try using different vowel sounds, like ooooh, and eeeeeh.

If you notice any spots that feel tense or uncomfortable, stop to give
them a little massage. If it feels good, roll your neck a little bit.
Try bending over to stretch out your back and legs or bending to the sides to
open your ribs and waist. Open your mouth really wide and then close it.
Play with your voice in any ways that feel good while you're stretching.

This warm-up stretches your muscles, relaxes your mind,
and helps connect your voice to your body.

Sirening & Movement
From Chapter 10, page 107. Tracks 9 & 10, Video # 4

With your feet solidly planted on the floor, or your bottom solidly planted
on your chair, inhale, raising your arms up in front of you. When you are full of
breath, your arms will be above your head, reaching up towards the sky.

As you begin to exhale, bring your arms back down, making an "Ahhh" sound.
Start with a high pitch when your hands are up and lower your pitch
as you lower your arms.

Bring to mind a child who is making the sound of a fire engine siren,
and begin to move from an "aahhh" sound to an "ooooh" or an "eeeee" sound.
Give it some power and volume and be sure to take in
a lot of breath on your inhales.

**Comfortably illustrate your sound with any movement
of your hands, arms or whole body as you siren and swoop your voice
up and down and up and down. Make a high pitch
when your motions go high, and a low pitch when your motions go low.**

**Play with it, keeping your hands, arms and body involved,
but now move and sing in whatever way you want.
Follow your impulses.**

Notice the sensations and vibrations in your body, throat, and face
as your voice sirens up and down. How does the air around you feel?

In the beginning you may have to focus to keep your motions and voice in sync
as you move up and down, but after you've done this for a little while
let go of any worry about whether you're getting it right or wrong.
Keep your consciousness as much in the present as possible.
Be curious.

Floppy Twist
From Chapter 10, Page 108. Video # 5
(Note: Stop or hold onto something if you start to feel dizzy!)

Stand and feel your weight solidly on the ground.
Imagine your weight and your energy extending down through your feet
into the center of the earth so that you are totally rooted.

Allow your knees to bend a little and begin to twist gently from side to side.
Gradually let your twist grow in size, keeping your arms loose and floppy
so that they swing around too, and flop against your body
like empty coat sleeves.

Include your head in the twist.
Inhale as you face front and exhale each time you twist around to the back.
Your breaths will be light and short, energetic but relaxed,
with a little puff on the exhale.

Begin to illustrate your twists with a little sound.
You might say "whap" as your hands flop against your body,
or "pahh" or "uhhh."
Take a break if you feel dizzy — I don't want you to fall down!

This is a good way to loosen up the muscles in your waist and ribcage,
and to relax your arms, shoulders and neck.
It also creates an energized and powerful breath,
and engages your voice in a way that's
very connected to your movement.

Neck Roll & Face Stretch
(Skip Step 1 if you have reason to think this will bother your neck.)

Step 1
Gently and slowly, roll your head to the front, sides and back to stretch your neck.
Modify this as needed.

Step 2
Open your mouth really wide, as if you were having a huge uninhibited yawn,
or as if you were a wild tiger. Then scrunch up your face and lips as if you'd just
tasted a lemon for the first time. Alternate these two moves a couple of times.
Finish off with a big wide smile.

Floor Stretches and Vocal Warm-Up

Lie down on your back on the floor or on a bed.
Stretch out a little bit: alternately arch and flatten your back;
hug your knees up to your chest and give a little squeeze;
lean your knees over to one side and then the other
to stretch out your waist and ribs.

Still lying down, start to move your arms in the air
and illustrate their movements with your voice.

Be as grounded and expressive as you can, keeping your arm movements
and breathing connected to your vocalization,
and see where this warm up takes you.

Side Stretch with Voice
From Chapter 10, page 109. Video #6

Stand or sit as in the Floppy Twist from page 215.

Reach up with your right arm, as though a string was pulling you up
through your middle finger as you reach for the sky.
Feel a nice stretch all along your right side, in your hip, waist,
ribs, neck, arm and hand. Bend a little to the left.

Breathe in and out deeply as you stretch,
and as you exhale, make any sounds that feel natural.
The job of your voice right now is to massage, from the inside,
any spots that need a little extra help releasing.

Repeat on the other side.

Neck, Jaw and Face Massage

Bring your attention to your shoulders, neck, jaw and face
and notice where you feel any tension.
Staying as relaxed as you can, use your hands to give those spots a nice massage.

Imagine that the hands at work are not yours.
Experiment with different amounts of pressure.

Voice and Breath Warm-Ups

Sss-sss-sss-sss-sss-sss-sss ...
From Chapter 12, page 121. Video #7

Try to include this in every warm-up;
it's a very effective way to remind your body how to breathe for singing.

Take a big relaxed breath and release it with short repeated ssss sounds
until your breath is used up. Notice which parts of your body are engaged
and working as you do this.

Check in to be sure your shoulders, neck and jaw are relaxed;
they should not be working hard at all.
Now place your hand over your the top of your belly.
Again, exhale on a series of short ssss sounds until you are out of air.

Notice how the muscles under your hand are contracting and releasing
with each ssss sound. These are the muscles that should be working!

These are your diaphragmatic muscles; you can distictly feel them working
in this exercise. Do this a few more times until you are able to clearly identify
what this diaphragmatic action feels like. If you are having trouble,
try exaggerating the action by squeezing in a little bit more with the muscles
under your hand while exhaling on the ssss sound.

If you are still unclear, try doing this in front of a mirror
to give yourself a visual cue.

Next, do a long "sssssssss" and as you approach the end of your breath
notice how hard you have to squeeze your stomach and diaphragm
to keep the ssss sound going. It's amazing how much breath
you have on reserve when you push with
those diaphragmatic muscles!

This exercise reminds your mind and your body that
your power for singing is coming from the diaphragm and core,
and not from the throat, jaw, etc. If you engage the diaphramatic muscles,
even lightly, when you sing (when you're singing you don't need to work them
nearly as hard as you are in this exercise), you will have more stamina, volume,
flexibility and fun. And it will be much easier to relax the rest of your body
so you'll feel more comfortable while you are singing.

Beginner's Mind – Beginner's Voice
From Chapter 10, page 109.

Lie on the floor and take a few quiet breaths. Enjoy the silence.

With a relaxed and curious attitude begin to hum quietly with your mouth closed,
noticing very closely the difference between the feel of the silence
and the feel of sound. Notice where in your body you feel the hum.
In your chest? Your throat? Inside your ears or your mouth?
Do you feel the vibration in your cheeks?

Also pay attention to any emotions, associations, memories or images
that come up. Try moving the hum up and down in pitch and notice
any changes. Try different volumes and notice any changes.
If you have any urge to rock or move your body, go with it.

This is a great way to wake up your voice —
the hum is a perfect segue from silence to sound.

Improvising With a Drone
From Chapter 14, page 146. Tracks 23 and 24

Here's another fantastic activity that gets your body
and soul into the singing groove.

You'll need either an instrument that can produce a long steady note,
a companion to sing with, or you can sing along with Tracks 23 and 24.

Start by singing along with the drone, on the same note.
Don't worry if you're not sure whether you're getting it right,
just find a note that feels to you like it's the same.

Slide your voice up and down, above and below the drone note,
using it as your home base and returning to it often.
Notice what it's like when your voice is clashing with the drone
versus when it's in harmony with the drone.
Don't think about clashing as bad and harmony as good — it's all good.

Follow your voice wherever it wants to go, exploring all the colors,
nuance and beauty that you are creating.

Doodling Around Home Base

Open your mouth and without thinking, sing one long note.
Whatever note appears becomes your home base for this exercise.
For a few breaths, drone on this note.

Then slide your voice up the tiniest bit and back again to the home base note; do this a few times. Next, slide just a tiny bit under the home base note and back again. Slowly expand your range out a little further, but return frequently to home base.

Create a little song (this is just for you — no worries about whether it's "good" or not), centered around the same home base note. Begin to stretch higher and lower in pitch, placing the highest and lowest notes of your song just a little further away from where you've been hanging out; you're gradually expanding your range, but the original long tone remains the home base for your composition.
Once you feel satisfied (or bored) with your song, start a new one with a home base note that's just a little higher.

This is an incredibly organic way of stretching out and waking up your vocal apparatus and getting your voice ready to sing whatever notes might be coming next.

And it's a great way to get centered.
When you're doing this exercise you're asking yourself, "Who am I musically, right now?" Returning again and again to the home base note gives you just enough structure to create a melody that is cohesive and musical, and totally your own.

Listening and Responding Expressively
From Chapter 11, page 114
(Chapter 11's more nuanced description will help you deepen this simple activity.)

Put on some recorded music and sing and dance along with it.

When doing this as a warm-up, start by only humming or singing the notes of the song that feel most comfortable. Don't feel you have to hit the highest or lowest notes right away, but rather creep up on them gradually, singing only what feels easily accessible.

As you continue to sing you will probably gain more and more accuracy but don't worry about it, just have fun. You'll be warming up your voice without "working" at it!

Heys

From Chapter 12, page 125. Track 11, Video #9

Don't do Heys until after you've done some gentler warm-ups.
Have a glass of water handy.

Stand or sit comfortably, with good alignment, and take in a nice full belly breath.
Look, or imagine looking, at a far away spot (across the street, across a river,
a canyon or a field for example; whatever works for you).

Call out, on any pitch, "Heeyyyy!" Don't scream or strain,
just relax and let out your natural voice in a big way.
Try "Heyyy Youuuuuu.....!" and let your voice trail away.
Do it as loud as you would if you were trying to get the attention of a friend
who's far away enough to look really small. "Heeeeyyyyy!"
Think "calling" rather than "singing." This is relaxed, but loud.

If you need to clear your voice, do it very gently or take a sip of water.
A little of this goes a long way — just a few times may be plenty.

Now, when you go into your regular singing, you'll have access to more range,
more volume, and to that joyous, out there, Hey energy.

Sirening

Sirening is basically just sliding your voice around from one pitch to another.
There are so many ways to do this and when you're warming up it's best
to do it in whatever way feels nicest to you in the moment.

Here are some approaches to try:

• Reach your hands up high over your head and siren from high
to low as you bring them down to your sides; your voice can be
soft and breathy or focused and narrow.

• Move your hand in front of you in the shape of the bottom half
of a circle. Your motion will look like the motion of a child
on a swing. Siren your voice in a way that imitates that motion.

• Imagine that you're a little kid pretending to be a fire engine.
Better yet, find an actual little kid and pretend you're fire engines
together. Make fire engine noises.

• Use the quietest of all voices to create a lullaby out of a siren.

*The next three warm-up exercises are great
for people who tend to run out of breath.
They will help train you to conserve
your breath while singing.*

Lip Trills with Sirens

Also called a rasberry. Put two fingers on each cheek, push up just a little bit, keep
your lips closed but relaxed. Blow out and bubble your lips, and vocalize.
While you're trilling, gently siren your voice up and down.

It's not always easy to get your lips vibrating (even though little kids
don't seem to have a hard time with it). You have to be sure to give just
the right and steady amount of air — which is part of what makes this a good
exercise — it teaches you to control air flow. Use your diaphragmatic breathing.

This silly activity has many other benefits: Like the "SS-SS-ss-ss" exercise,
it brings your body's attention to the diaphramatic muscles.
It also helps to release tension in the face and mouth.

Hum on a Vvvvvvv Shape

In this exercise you'll gently siren with your mouth in the V position,
(the position you'd put your mouth into when you say the word "Vocal").

This position won't let you expel your breath very quickly,
so when you do this it teaches your body what it feels like to vocalize
while releasing air more slowly and steadily.

Don't push the air out in bursts but rather look for consistency in air pressure.

Hum with Your Tongue Sticking Out

That's about it.
This is another exercise that teaches breath consistency.
This exercise also stretches your tongue.

Babbling With Articulation

Make as many articulate sounds, using vowels separated by specific consonants,
as fast as you possibly can. For example I might say,
"tikatikatikabidibidibidibidibidimanamanamanamanalulululudodadodadida,"
but it would just be popping out before I could possibly think about it,
and I would never be able to reconstruct what I did.
So much of what we're doing in this book is slow and contemplative,
and babbling this way is a great counterpoint to that.

If singing "heys" breaks the sound barrier (see page 125),
babbling breaks the self-censorship barrier.
Babbling pushes you to a speed where your sounds are coming out faster
than your thoughts can possibly control them, allowing you to access
your imagination in a soley intuitive way.

Bobbie McFerrin, singer and vocal percussionist extrordinaire, suggests that his
students do this for two minutes every day for a year and see what happens.
Your skill at articulation will improve and your creative juices will be released.

Babbling also stretches and exercises the inside of your mouth and tounge,
and trains you to make speedy shifts with your voice.

From the collections of the Imperial War Museums.
The Oxford and Bermondsey Boys' Clubs London, December, 1943

Ear and Voice Tuning Warm-Ups

Sing a Song You Like

Singing a familiar song is a great warm-up as long as it doesn't have notes that are at the bottom or top of your range.

If you're not already warmed up it's better to sing a song that is in a comfortable and fairly limited range. It's interesting to start by singing a song low, and then to sing the same song again a little higher, and again a little higher, discovering how high you're able to move the song as you get warmed up.

Sliding and Improvising Against a Drone
From Chapter 14, page 146, Tracks 23 and 24

Here it is again! Great for a voice warm-up but also great for ear training.

I describe this exercise in many places because there is almost nothing that singing with a drone isn't good for!

Sing (And Repeat) Random Intervals

Sing back and forth between any two distinct notes. This is different from sirening, where you are moving slowly between the notes and focusing on hearing all the pitches inbetween.

Here, you are sustaining one note and then going straight to another note and sustaining that one, and then repeating. Give yourself a long enough time with each interval to nail each note.

Notice how this feels and sounds. Now change just one of the notes and go back and forth between those two notes a few times. Notice the ways in which this feels and sounds different from the first set of notes. Spend a little time with this, always moving just one of the notes.

Try starting with a close interval and then moving gradually to wider and wider intervals.

Sing What You Play

This is for any instrumentalist except for those who play wind instruments
(although it may be fun to try blowing and singing at the same time).
Even if you don't really play an instrument but have one available to use,
you will benefit from this warm-up. If you're a musician, this fosters a
deep connection between your voice and your instrument, and allows your
already existing musicianship to help you out as a singer.
(And vice versa. Your new singing abilities
can help you to go deeper as an instrumentalist.)

Play a note on your instrument, and then match that note with your voice.
Do this at various pitches, not only matching the note, but imitating
the quality of the sound of your instrument. Play, then sing. Play, then sing.
When you've mastered this, build up the number of notes you can play/sing,
until you're playing and then singing little phrases.

Another variation is to anticipate the note that will come from your instrument
and sing what you're playing as close to simultaneously as possible.
This is more difficult for most people, so start with just single notes
and short pairs of 2 notes, and build up from there.

*This exercise, as well as Babbling with Articulation, are fundamental exercises that
I learned at "Music for People," an organization that gives music
improvisation workshops. Learn about Music for People
in Appendix IV: Resources.*

Sing Parts of the Diatonic Scale
From Chapter 16, page 157. Tracks 29-33

Use the audio track or a piano keyboard for support.
Unless you understand how to move scales around on the piano, play in the
key of C, with the C note being the 1, so you only need to play white notes.

Start with the 1 and 2 notes of the scale you're in; go back and forth between them.
It may take you a while to sing that accurately. When you're
confident with that, try singing 1-2-3 forwards and then backwards.
Next, try working on 1-2-3-4-5, but if those notes feel too tricky, explore the 1-3-5
intervals instead; those note combinations can be more intuitive, easier to learn,
and more useful for beginning singers than learning the whole scale.

Finally, you may be able to sing the whole scale: 1-2-3-4-5-6-7-8. Yay!
And backwards: 8-7-6-5-4-3-2-1. And using the words Do-Re-Mi-Fa-So-La-Ti-Do.

The *Do-Re-Mi* song from the movie *The Sound of Music* may have more
meaning to you after you've mastered singing scales yourself.
I recommend you get some popcorn and check it out.

Sing Variations of 1-3-5-8
From Chapter 16, page 158. Tracks 33-36

Sing various combinations of the 1-3-5-8 notes of the diatonic scale.
This helps your brain and vocal apparatus remember how the notes
in our western scale relate to each other, builds muscle memory and agility,
and makes it easier to sing in tune.

There are endless variations on singing the 1-3-5-8. Here are a few ...

• Sing it with your tongue sticking out or with your mouth positioned in the
"v" shape (as in "vocal"). This way you're also practicing breath control.

• Sing it on the sound of "ng" as in Si"ng"! This closes off the back of your
throat and exercises the back of your tongue.

• Sing it saying gug-gug-gug — this helps you become more definitive and
confident about your pitches because you can't slide into that hard
G consonant; when you're off you can hear it and when you're on it's
very satisfying.

More 1-3-5-8 Variations
From Chapter 16, page 158. Tracks 35 & 36

Sing the 1-3-5-8 notes forwards and backwards (1-3-5-8-5-3-1)
with your own words, or try these:
"I Can Sing High And Sing Low"
"I Love to Sing Love to Sing"
"You Are So Tall I Am Short"
"Look at the Sky and the Ground"
"What a Nice Hat and Nice Shoes"

You can also hang out longer on the 8 note, like this:
1-3-5-8-8-8-8-5-3-1

Sing it using a variety of real and made up words:
Ma-ma-ma, ba-ba-ba, da-da-da!
Play around with it. Make stuff up.

Sing 1-3flat-5 (From the Minor Diatonic Scale)
From Chapter 16, page 159, Tracks 37

You can do all the same warm-ups as above except with a flatted 3,
which means that you are singing a minor scale, which has a whole different feel.
This makes for a very nice and soulful warm-up.

Your warm-ups aren't just exercises to go through in a rote manner.
They are not just physical; they are also intellectual and emotional.
They are for stretching your muscles and vocal cords, deepening your breath,
and for reminding your mind and body what it feels like to support
your voice with your breathing and to sing specific intervals.
And they are, just as importantly, for getting in the zone and feeling the love.

Your warm-up is the transition time between the rest of your day
and the singing part of your day. It's your vessel of safe passage, a place where you
have the opportunity to reconnect with the beauty of your voice,
and the calming, revitalizing massage of its vibration.

Enjoy your warm-up as you would a hot bath on a cold winter's evening,
or a cool dip in a lake on a hot summer's day. Let your warm-up be a special treat!

Appendix II
Handy-Dandy Warm-Up Tear-Out Sheet

Full Body Warm-Ups

Yoga Stretch with Breath and Sound
Sirening & Movement
Floppy Twist
Neck Roll & Face Stretch
Floor Stretches and Vocal Warm-Up
Side Stretch
Neck, Jaw and Face Massage

Voice and Breath Warm-Ups

Sss-sss-sss-sss-sss-sss-sss
Beginner's Mind — Beginner's Voice
Improvising With a Drone
Doodling Around Home Base
Listening and Responding Expressively
Heys
Sirening
Lip Trills with Sirens
Hum on a Vvvvvvvv Shape
Hum with Your Tongue Sticking Out
Babbling With Articulation

Ear and Voice Tuning Warm-Ups

Sing a Song You Like
Sliding and Improvising Against a Drone
Sing (And Repeat) Random Intervals
Sing What You Play
Sing Parts of the Diatonic Scale
Sing Variations of 1-3-5-8
More 1-3-5-8 Variations
Sing 1-3flat-5 (From the Minor Diatonic Scale)

Fear of Singing Breakthrough Program • www.FearOfSinging.com

Appendix III
Practice Session Ideas Tear-Out Sheet

A practice session can last hours or take just a few minutes.
Below are ideas that can be used with the "Club Sandwich" practice model (page 190).
Mix and match these ideas according to how much time you have and the mood you're in.
Let every practice session be as musical, playful, beautiful,
expressive, and fun as it can be!

START WITH SOMETHING EASY

• Loosen up by humming, sirening, or making some crazy sounds.

• Engage your body with a stretching and breathing warm-up.

• Sing a familiar song that comes easily and that you enjoy.

DO SOMETHING MORE CHALLENGING

• Practice specific intervals using a piano or a recording, or do it with a friend.

• Spend a few minutes working on learning a song.

(It's okay to get a little bit frustrated but not TOO frustrated)
If you're getting too frustrated ...

DO SOMETHING FUN AND EASY; MOVE AROUND

• Get up and walk around or do something else relaxing for a minute or two.

• Put on a drone and improvise to it — sing something expressive.

• Put on a favorite song and dance and sing along with it. Stretch. Breathe.

Meanwhile the activity that was getting frustrating may have jelled somewhat
in your subconscious so when you return to it again it's easier.

DO SOMETHING MORE CHALLENGING

• Now maybe it's time to go back to the intervals or the challenging song
that you were working on before. See if a little audiating helps.

• Or pick up something else that you find somewhat challenging.

FINISH UP WITH SOMETHING FUN, EASY, AND SATISFYING

Do something that makes you happy — remember why you want to learn to sing!
Remember that singing can touch your soul. Try one of the following:

• Get more expressive with a song you're working on, or try out a new song.

• Get a tapping rhythm going on a drum or a table and improvise a song
with that rhythm as your accompaniment.

• Sing loud or dramatically.

Fear of Singing Breakthrough Program   • www.FearOfSinging.com

Appendix IV
Resources

This is an informal collection of resources that have meant
a lot to me and that I think you might find useful.
Visit www.FearOfSinging.com/book1 for links to many of these resources.

Psychology, Mindset and Meditation

Pema Chodron has written many approachable and inspirational books about meditation including the primer, *How to Meditate*.

John Kabat Zinn, author of the books *Full Catastrophe Living*, and *Mindfulness Meditation in Everyday Life and Exercises & Meditations*, has also made some excellent recordings with guided meditations that I have liked very much.

Brené Brown has produced many books, ebooks, lectures and ecourses around the subjects of shame resilience, daring living, and more. I very much enjoyed the audiobook: *Men, Women and Worthiness: The Experience of Shame and the Power of Being Enough*.

The Artist's Way by **Julia Cameron** has helped many people, including myself, break through blocks to free their creativity. A wonderful book/workbook for all kinds of artists, and anybody looking to discover their artist within.

Love is the Killer App, **Tim Sanders**. This terrific book is ostensibly just about business, but I found that its message extended into life in general.

Songbooks and Books about Music and/or Singing

Rise Up Singing, by **Peter Blood & Annie Patterson**. Truly the bible of songbooks for group singing, this book is full of songs you and your friends are sure to know and love. It includes lyrics and guitar chords — if you need help remembering the tunes you can look them up online.

Rise Again: A Group Singing Songbook, by **Peter Blood & Annie Patterson**. The much awaited sequel to *Rise Up Singing*.

Singing in the African American Tradition, by **Ysaye Barnwell**, is an instructional book/CD set for learning to sing African songs and African American spirituals and gospel songs. Barnwell teaches the melody and harmony parts by ear, so a group can share the book or buy several, and make some amazing music together.

Rounds Galore, by **Sol Weber.** This is Part 1 of an extensive collection of rounds, many of which are quite simple. (This is from their website: "Teaching children Harmony? Teaching adults the Joy of Singing? Want something fun for a long trip with the kids? Looking for the perfect gift for a singer-friend? Rounds are the fastest way to get kids and adults singing in harmony!")

The Listening Book, **W.A. Mathieu.** This beautifully written guide into deep listening is poetic, meditative and inspirational.

Return to Child, The Music for People Improvisation Guide: Music for People's Guide to Improvising Music and Authentic Group Leadership, written and compiled by **James Oshinsky.** Philosophy, games, and techniques developed by David Darling, Bonnie Insull and participants in Music for People workshops. (See more about Music for People below.)

Innovative Drum Circles: Beyond Beat Into Harmony! by **Mary Knysh.** A very friendly, accessible guide to group music-making for educators, therapists, facilitators and music lovers. Illustrated step-by-step instructions for facilitating dynamic musical and rhythmic group experiences.

All Together Singing in the Kitchen: Creative ways to make & listen to music as a family, by **Nerissa Nields & Katryna Nields.** Lots of fun — this book will help any family become a musical family. Giving your kids or grandkids the gift of music is one of the best things you can do!

SpiritArts: Transformation through Creating Art, Music and Dance, by **Lynn Miller.** A beautiful book about how the arts connect to the soul, and enhance well-being. Full of exercises and ideas to put into practice.

Vocal River: The Skill and Spirit of Improvisation, by **Rhiannon.** Rhiannon is a big figure in the world of vocal improvisation, and her book is a rich resource for both the why and the how of it. She is one of the people who developed, along with Bobby McFerrin, a process called "Circle Singing" which is something people are now doing around the world. (See next page.)

Music/Singing Organizations & Opportunities

Music for People. Music improvisation workshops and trainings for "non-musicians" and very experienced musicians together. Imagine being a "non-musician" and yet being able to sit in a circle with, for example, a concert cellist, an electric bass player, an African drummer, and a jazz singer, and make beautiful music together. An orientation of non-judgement and play, along with simple techniques and games makes this amazing kind of experience happen at every workshop!

Music Together®. Music and movement classes for children aged 0-6 along with their parents or caregivers. Very tuned into child development, this program understands that children learn music through play and immersion, just the way they learn language. If you want to give the children in your life the gift of music, enrolling in this program is the way to do it! And here's the thing — you cannot take your child to these classes without also improving your own singing skills. It's inevitable. And really fun.

Tone Deaf Chorus or Choirs. My initial plan was tell you about **W.A. Mathieu's** *Tone Deaf Chorus,* as it was his *"The Listening Book,"* that introduced me to this concept. But now I see that these are popping up everywhere! There are some that teach people to sing, and others where people seem to be just chanting without focusing on improving their singing skills. They both seem like fun. If you find something happening near you I suggest you check it out!

Circle Singing. These are community vocal improvisation gatherings for anyone who enjoys singing. Inspired by Bobby McFerrin and his colleagues, participants use games and structures that make it easy to join in, creating interlocking bits of music right on the spot. If you're inspired you can try leading; if you're shy or inexperienced you can follow. Usually magic happens: beautiful harmonies, crazy sounds, powerful expression, laughing… always a delightful surprise. Ask around or go online to see if there is any Circle Singing happening near you!

Village Harmony. Multicultural singing programs, workshops and camps. With teachers from around the world, songs are taught with remarkable authenticity and awareness of their cultural context. Although there are no auditions, these camps are best for somewhat experienced singers. Here is a quote from their website and I quite agree: "Written music is distributed as appropriate, but many songs are taught solely by ear, and virtually everything is taught by example. Emphasis is placed on authenticity, not just on replication. Above all we strive for total conviction, and singing with joy. Intense as the days are, Village Harmony groups tend to be extremely relaxed, non-competitive and democratic in nature. The supportive and inclusive community at our camps is such that no one is afraid to give their all in performance and sing from the deepest place in their hearts."

More Great Organizations You Might Enjoy...

The Children's Music Network
People's Music Network
Country Song and Dance Society
The Center for Traditional Music and Dance (in NYC)
Playing for Change

Tools & Technology

(Go to www.fearofsinging/book1 for links.)
Online Piano
Online Metronome
Sing & See (Pitch Matching Software)
Shruti Box